Democracy
IN THE AGE OF
New Media

This book is part of the Peter Lang Media and Communication list.
Every volume is peer reviewed and meets
the highest quality standards for content and production.

PETER LANG
New York • Washington, D.C./Baltimore • Bern
Frankfurt • Berlin • Brussels • Vienna • Oxford

Tauel Harper

Democracy IN THE AGE OF New Media

The Politics of the Spectacle

PETER LANG

New York • Washington, D.C./Baltimore • Bern
Frankfurt • Berlin • Brussels • Vienna • Oxford

Library of Congress Cataloging-in-Publication Data

Harper, Tauel.
Democracy in the age of new media: The politics of the spectacle /
Tauel Harper.
p. cm.
Includes bibliographical references and index.
1. Mass media—Political aspects. 2. Citizenship. I. Title.
P95.8.H37   306.2—dc22   2010030330
ISBN 978-1-4331-0911-9 (hardcover)
ISBN 978-1-4331-0910-2 (paperback)

Bibliographic information published by **Die Deutsche Nationalbibliothek**.
Die Deutsche Nationalbibliothek lists this publication in the "Deutsche
Nationalbibliografie"; detailed bibliographic data is available
on the Internet at http://dnb.d-nb.de/.

Cover image: *Untitled*, by Erin Coates.
Pencil and paint on photographic print
© 2010 Erin Coates, http://erincoates.net

The paper in this book meets the guidelines for permanence and durability
of the Committee on Production Guidelines for Book Longevity
of the Council of Library Resources.

Contents

Acknowledgments

This book is the culmination of many years research and much work on behalf of a number of people to whom I'm greatly indebted. I would like to thank Peter Lang and particularly Mary Savigar and Sophie Appel for their support in the creation and production of this work. I'd also particularly like to thank Kawan Publications for their wonderful assistance in readying the manuscript for print.

Much of the research for this book derived from my PhD research completed while at Murdoch University. My gratitude to my PhD supervisor Ian Cook and colleagues such as David Brown and Yvonne Haigh remains undiminished, as does my appreciation of Lubica and Lenka Ucnik for first introducing me to Hannah Arendt. I also appreciate the attentive feedback of Douglas Kellner, Rodney Smith and Graham Maddox, whose comments on my early research helped me refine this work. My colleagues at UWA also deserve my thanks for being so supportive over the last three years. In particular the support and friendship of David Savat, Stewart Woods, Larissa Sexton-Fink, David Denemark, Leonie Harris, Linda Cresswell, Ines Bortolini and Hui Chuin Poa has been integral to the completion of this book. My friends and colleagues Helen Merrick and John Corner have provided crucial support and advice at important times over the course of this project and Erin Coates graciously let me use her artwork for the cover. I would also like to thank my students, who have been a constant source of inspiration and pride.

Finally, I would like to thank my personal support network. Firstly, my wife Kate, who gets me out of my cave and smiling at the world. Secondly, my friends who have supported me well beyond the pale of sanity or reciprocity—thanks so much. My father and sister are heroes of mine, as people who strive to consider and live the best life possible and I appreciate that, along with my sweet grandparents, they have always been there for me. But it is my mother, Gail Harper, who deserves my deepest gratitude. From teaching me to read as a child to providing extensive advice and proofreading for this book, she has shown kindness, intelligence and understanding which has inspired my engagement with politics and communication. I will never be able to repay her generosity but as a small token of my appreciation I dedicate this book to her.

Credits for Lyrics and Artwork

The Concept of Democracy

A pure democracy is a society consisting of a small number of citizens, who assemble and administer the government in person.

—James Madison

Democracy is a deceptively simple concept—rule by the people. What "rule by the people" means is far more difficult to discern. Some believe that democracy means people should be actively engaged in the process of government, while others suggest it means that the people should act as a critical judge of the political process, entitled to vote out the government if it fails to do its job. Regardless of what you assume democracy to mean, it is hard to argue that people in advanced industrial economies are getting better at democracy unless you insist that democracy has little to do with politics. There are a number of reasons to suggest that the great democratic governments do not actually allow for rule by the people; that instead, representative democracy merely creates the illusion of choice and control, all the while further entrenching the interests of the already powerful. If "rule by the people" refers to individuals' participation in decisions about what is shared and public, then contemporary political systems have only a tenuous claim to be democratic.

Despite the widespread acceptance of representative democracy as the best political system, it is unusual to find anyone living in that system who feels like they have a personal role to play in the process of government. When it comes to important political decisions it seems that the individual has very little say in what the government does. Instead, it seems many individuals feel as though the political system is thoroughly divorced from their everyday lives and, in many cases, that they are powerless to change anything politically. As a result they turn away from politics and voting altogether, and turn towards more responsive and gratifying ways of expressing their self-rule.

This disenchantment with politics has a number of important ramifications. Firstly, the decline in political engagement suggests there will be a corresponding decline in the public scrutiny of political decisions. Secondly, such a decline undermines the idea that the political system is a place to showcase the best people and ideas of democratic culture, meaning that the political system no longer inspires public thought and action. Finally, the absence of the opportunity to display one's values, identity and contribution in public means that individuals are far more likely to invest this display in private, or quasi-private settings. As such, the failure of people to engage with democratic politics renders contemporary democracies as a pallid incarnation of "rule by the people".

Presiding over this move away from politics are the media. Long conceived as the "Fourth Estate", a fundamental tool for facilitating communication between the political sphere and the general public, the role of the media in fostering this communication, or in many cases, stifling it, is becoming ever more apparent. It is clear that in a representative democracy, the media ought to play a central role in relating political issues to the citizens and citizens' concerns to the politicians. However, we find that the media are decreasing their coverage of politics and, instead, increasingly emphasising private issues—such as material wealth, personal safety and entertainment as the really important aspects of our daily life.

How is it that representative democracies can maintain so much faith in government while distancing the people from the activity of self-rule? The answer is through the staging of spectacles. Spectacles are those moments when our attention is drawn towards things that are sensational, engaging and stimulating. Spectacles are staged for our enjoyment, to gain our attention and employ it to add to the benefit of those doing the staging. All the time spectacles serve to take our attention away from the reality of what we still share. The societies of advanced industrial economies are dominated by spectacles—events and spaces where citizens' attention is diverted away from what is public towards what is entertaining and gratifying.

This book provides an explanation of how changes in both politics and media technology have led to the erosion of democratic values and, subsequently, it explores the need to reinvent democratic practices. It explores the effects of media saturation on politics and society. It seeks to explain how the traditional role of the citizen has been fundamentally altered by the influence of the media on the public sphere. This media influence, it is argued, has resulted in an alienation from the "public" life and an increased prominence of private concerns among individuals. A few notable effects of this change in the expectations of individuals have been a declining interest in the world of political institutions, a rise of a celebrity culture and an economy which primarily produces waste. This book seeks to explain how this situation has developed, outline what effect it has on both people and democratic systems, and explore some of the positive possibilities of a spectacular democracy.

Agonistic and Deliberative Democratic Theory

The contemporary critique of democracy and the standard of public communication has been defined by two broad schools of political philosophy. On the one hand there are those who criticise democratic systems for failing to open up political decisions to sufficient public scrutiny. This group has been defined as advocates of the deliberative school and includes commentators such as Jurgen Habermas and Craig Calhoun. On the other hand are those who criticise democratic systems for their failure to actively engage and inspire individuals. This group can be defined as agonistic democrats and are lead by theorists such as Hannah Arendt and Chantal Mouffe. The deliberative school has a tendency to focus on developing decision making processes so that they are reasonable and legitimate, whereas the agonistic school has a tendency to focus on personal engagement with the political process, to ensure that participation is open, equitable and inspiring.

While much has been made by political theorists about the differences between these two schools of democratic theory, the position put forward in this book is that when thinking about actually existing democracy, they have more in common with each other than they have differences. In order to explore this similarity, I shall be using the theories developed by Hannah Arendt from the agonistic school and Jurgen Habermas from the deliberative school. I've chosen Habermas and Arendt because they are each prolific and highly respected exponents of each school. While they do not encapsulate the full variety of agonistic and deliberative views, they are somewhat emblematic of their schools and their extensive writing allows a detailed analysis of the philosophical underpinnings of their democratic theories. Finally, Habermas and Arendt share a common understanding about the manner in which power operates within society, which makes their theories particularly useful for understanding the effect of media upon contemporary democracy—that being that power is constituted through communication.

The Concept of Communicative Power

Deliberative and agonistic theorists share the view that power is constituted through the process of communication. A brief introduction to the concept of communicative power serves to identify what deliberative and agonistic theorists base their principles upon and why representative democracy poses such a threat to the rule of the people. The communicative understanding of power differs from the traditional understanding of power as it based on the assumption that the realm of action available to an individual is not just constrained by direct physical control of their action, but also and more generally through constraining what it is possible for an individual to say, think and do in a given situation. This understanding of power forms the basis of this book's critique of democracy and provides for a sophisticated understanding of media effects.

Power can be understood to be the capacity to effect action. The typical liberal understanding of power focuses on the freedom of individual actions— if the action of an individual is restrained in any way, then the individual is subject to power. Liberal democracy, as a result, focuses on allowing the individual the utmost freedom from restraint. The concept of communicative power, on the other hand, suggests that the capacity to effect action is equally enabled through shared agreement that that action is valid, real and achievable. At the basis of this understanding is a belief that the capacity to act is largely shaped by the communicative situation in which one acts.

The idea that power operates through communication has long been asserted by communicative theorists; notably Roland Barthes, Judith Butler, Michel Foucault and Umberto Eco. Of these, Foucault is most renowned for developing the concept of discourses as the conduits of communicative power. Discourses "define, describe [and] delimit what it is possible to say (and by extension what it is possible to do or not to do)" (Kress 1988, p. 160). By taking part in discourses, individuals also take part in the construction of power: "Power is everywhere; not just because it embraces everything but because it comes from everywhere...Power comes from below" (Foucault 1978, p. 94).

The concept of communicative power is based upon the notion that power is collectively produced within a communicative community. That is to say, in the process of reasoning, the power of our convictions stands and falls according to the *mutual* acknowledgement that these convictions are acceptable to the wider community (Habermas 1983, p. 173). Arendt expresses this understanding of mutual acknowledgement as the basis of power throughout her work.

> It is the people's support that lends power to the institutions of a country, and this support is but the continuation of the consent that brought the laws into existence to begin with...All political institutions are manifestations and materializations of power; they petrify and decay as soon as the living power of the people ceases to uphold them.[1]

The communicative element of this notion of power is derived from the element of community that is central to it. Arendt argues that "when we taste or judge, we judge in our role as a 'member of a community'" (Arendt 1978b, p. 72). By this she means that we share communicative presuppositions that determine judgements and statements to be relevant and appropriate. It is only within the common bonds of shared understanding that it is possible to manifest power: "While strength is the natural quality of the individual seen in isolation, power springs up between men when they act together and vanishes the moment they disperse" (Arendt 1958, p. 200). According to Arendt, the public is constituted through people speaking and acting together, and in this fundamental way she commits herself to the investigation of communicative power.

Habermas flags his general approval of Arendt's understanding of the communicative aspect of power in an admiring article about her work (Habermas 1977)[2]. In this piece Habermas contends that Arendt shares his understanding of power as that which "corresponds to the human ability not just to act, but to act in concert" (Arendt 1970, p. 41). This reflects Habermas's own understanding of power stemming from the force of reason. Habermas also notes that Arendt similarly advocates a democratic system based around the legitimate and equitable process of public communication (Habermas 1983, p. 183). In making this proclamation Habermas identifies two important resonances between his own work and that of Arendt. First, he recognises that Arendt shares his view that power is communicatively generated. Second, he acknowledges that Arendt's political philosophy also reflects a desire to reconcile institutions of power with this communicative power through the public use of reason.

Due to this understanding Habermas and Arendt also agree that the public ought to serve a critical function, providing a forum for criticism and the refinement of communicative power through discussion. This shared understanding is based upon the Socratic principle that when one seeks to determine what is real, the more opinions that are consulted, the more "real" the final estimation of reality will be[3]. This element of Arendt's thought can most adequately be summed up in the following statement:

> Only where things can be seen by many in a variety of aspects without changing their identity, so that those who are gathered around them know they see sameness in utter diversity, can worldly reality truly and reliably appear. (Arendt 1958, p. 57)

This implies that the process of ascertaining "reality" requires exposure to publicity in order to prove its authenticity. Given this, the importance of the quality of public debate—who gets to take part in it and how it is conducted—

becomes an inherently political and important issue as this public debate determines what is considered to be "real". To put the problem a little too simply, if the political system teaches people to act as consumers, we cannot be surprised if people understand consumption to be the most publicly important activity. What Arendt and Habermas hope for is a political system which teaches people to think and act publicly, so that democracy regains its critical and expressive aspects.

It is in outlining the first priorities of public debate that deliberative and agonistic theorists differ. Deliberative theorists emphasise the processes necessary to ensure that reality is objective, reasonable or legitimate whereas agonistic theorists emphasise the importance of ensuring that the public forum is as open and inclusive as possible. While there are certainly some differences between the two democratic theories as a result, their shared understanding of communicative power suggests that their democratic theories are far more complementary than they are conflicting. This book highlights this complementary nature of deliberative and agonistic theories. By highlighting how public expression and public thought are intrinsically related, this book provides a comprehensive account of the problems with democracy and presents some possible solutions to those problems.

Overview of the Book

This book is divided into three main parts, with each part operating independently but combining to provide an overarching account of how media technologies have effected changes in public life.

The first part "Critical Reflections on Modern Democracy" acts as an introduction to the important theories employed to understand what has gone wrong with contemporary democracy. To this end it outlines the two major schools of critical democratic theory—the agonistic school and the deliberative school. By highlighting these schools' criticisms of modern democracy, it is possible to paint a clear picture of why democracy can be seen to be, in many senses, failing its duty to cater to the sovereignty of individuals. The first chapter focuses on the democratic theory of the agonistic school—and particularly the work of Hannah Arendt as the most prolific and comprehensive representative of that school. The chapter seeks to articulate the problem that agonists find with contemporary democracies—which is chiefly that the political system is too exclusive and not inspiring enough. Both of these factors result in a public forum which does not play the role it should; that is reconciling and celebrating individuality in a publicly constructive way.

The second chapter focuses on the democratic theory of the deliberative school through the work of the most prominent deliberative theorist—Jurgen Habermas. An investigation of Habermas's work highlights how representative democracy—particularly when operating in conjunction with a highly centralised mass media—can transform the public sphere from one where critical public issues are debated feverishly to one where political leadership need only *appear* consultative and democratic. This chapter goes on to describe the deliberative solution to this problem, which is to seek to institute ideal forms of communication in every aspect of social integration.

The final chapter of the first part of this book analyses how deliberative and agonistic theories can be understood to relate to changes in the media landscape. This chapter focuses on the transformation of the public sphere and the concurrent shift in media effects theories. Overall, the first part can be understood to be the theoretically intense portion of the book, which provides the background necessary to develop a more sophisticated analysis of the media's effect on democratic processes.

The second part of the book "Digital Spaces: Digital Selves" provides an account of how the changes in the public sphere described in the first part can be understood to lead to a new kind of individual and thus, a new form of public engagement. A central concern of Part Two is to identify how contemporary changes in public space and forms of communication have led to changes in the way individuals learn to behave. Chapter Four—Introducing the Age of the Spectacle—seeks to establish how the kinds of public space encountered by contemporary citizens are fundamentally different from those outlined in the first three chapters. In short, the loss of the legitimate and validating public realm leads to the development of a new kind of citizen—*homo spectaculum*—or being of the spectacle.

Chapter Five outlines the various public realms occupied by *homo spectaculum*. Through an investigation of the various systems of meaning with which *homo spectaculum* engages, it becomes clear that what is assumed to be public in the age of the spectacle is actually private space operating as public space. Such spaces are dominated by spectacles—that is dramatic events which entertain and occupy but which serve to distract and distance people from reality.

Part Three "Spectacular ®evolution: Democracy and the Spectacle" outlines how *homo spectaculum* interacts with representative democracy and introduces some possible outcomes of this interaction. Chapter Six details the fundamental incompatibility between the expressive power of *homo spectaculum* and the political system of representative democracy. It goes on to outline how this incompatibility is producing various systemic crises such as terrorism and economic collapse, and concludes by describing two of the possible futures suggested by this trajectory.

Chapter Seven explores the solution to these problems through a synthesis of Habermas's and Arendt's democratic theory. It explores the progressive aspects of *homo spectaculum* and focuses particularly on how developments in information and communication technologies can be understood to be facilitating the re-emergence of democracy. This discussion paves the way for the Conclusion which outlines what can be done to improve democratic systems and avoid a spectacular democratic failure.

This book provides an introduction to the transformative potential of public engagement and prompts critical reflection on how that public engagement is mediated. A large part of this book is critical of democracy as it is currently practised and laudatory of radical changes to democracy that encourage personal engagement in politics. This argument is based upon the understanding that the destructive tendencies of late capitalist societies and the degradation of democratic systems within these societies are inherently linked. Within the context of the "War on Terror", ecological disasters and the "Credit Crisis", this book does not hold up representative democracy as an ideal to be emulated, but rather calls for critical reflection about what kind of political culture we in the West are exporting, particularly given democracy's apparent failure to engage the communicative power of its own constituents.

PART ONE

CRITICAL REFLECTIONS ON MODERN DEMOCRACY

The Agonistic Public Realm

The two qualities that the slave, according to Aristotle, lacks—and it is because of these defects that he is not human—are the faculty to deliberate and decide and to foresee and choose.

—Hannah Arendt (1958: 84ft)

Agonistic democracy emphasises the virtues of direct political participation as the best way for people to express themselves. Through engaging with a public forum, people are not only able to express their identity but are concurrently able to critically engage in the construction of communicative power. Agonists believe that the motivation necessary to establish a polis arises directly from the human desire to have a common and "real" forum in which to express themselves. Reality, in turn, is constituted in the processes of public dialogue, display and storytelling. Agonistic theory suggests that the human need to make meaning means that we will always seek to share a public space. In order to explain this point, I shall describe the various functions of Arendt's ideal polis in fulfilling certain needs. Through identifying the display function of public appearance, Arendt provides valuable insights into the human energies that affirm democracy as the only form of government commensurate with human dignity.

An exploration of Arendt's ideal of agonistic politics serves to highlight some of the similarities between her ideal political discourse and that of Habermas. In both cases, power is understood to be communicatively constituted and democratic virtue is judged upon the amount of critical interaction that individuals have with the world around them. Arendt emphasises the various roles publics serve in validating personal identities and as a result it is possible to come to a better understanding of the ways in which the corruption of such publics can be understood to contribute to the corruption of individuals. At the same time, Arendt emphasises that people seek out such publics in order to generate meaning and thus she highlights the important role public space plays in locating our sense of "reality". The innate human desire for real meaning, such as that which can be constituted through public space, provides the central tenet of hope for those of us who wish to see democracy as an emancipative system.

This initial discussion of the political thought of Hannah Arendt is based largely upon her work *The Human Condition* (Arendt 1958). In this work Arendt presents a powerful criticism of modern democracies and outlines the philosophical foundations of this critique. For Arendt the most important aspect of public communication is that, when done well, it provides a way for people to express their individuality in a socially productive way. As a result, Arendt seeks to establish forums for communication which encourage self-expression. This, in turn, encourages self-reflection and a sense of ownership and belonging to the community. In order to make this clear, I shall briefly highlight how important critical thinking is to a healthy public realm before outlining how Arendt feels that *modern* public spaces act to limit critical thinking.

Underpinning this exploration is an awareness that democracy simply doesn't matter to people any more. Certainly, people still seek to express themselves and politics still happens, but the forms of expressive communication described in this chapter are no longer linked to democratic processes. Understanding the benefits of public communication and then thinking about how public communication has been usurped is the first step toward finding solutions to the problems of contemporary democracies.

Arendt and the Importance of Thinking

According to Arendt, humanity makes itself remarkable through the interrelated faculties of thought, speech and action. We are the only species we know of which is able to abstract ourselves away from our natural imperatives and, instead, base our lives on systems of power and belief facilitated through communication. The particular human faculties which give rise to this abstraction are those of thinking, speaking and acting. According to the theory of the communicative composition of power, it is the way we communicate which gives rise to the systems of power which define our actions. Given this, Arendt sees that the process of communication contributes to systems of power and the kind of thoughts people have. She does not see that people arrive in the world "fully formed" but rather that people develop themselves according to the traditions, spaces and systems with which they engage. In order to ensure that humans avoid being conditioned and restrained by these systems of power, she suggests that public spaces and systems should encourage people to think for themselves.

Arendt understands the ability to think to be the ability of a free human in a free society (Horowitz 1999, p. 273). Thinking and manifesting this thought through speech and action in the world is the unique characteristic of human existence that presents the possibility for glory. To avoid thinking is to go through life abiding by rules and norms without reflection, which is an aberration of the human condition. Life without thinking, acting and speaking would destroy the "potentialities of human power [and] dispossess us of all power [such that] we can repeat along with Jesus: 'It were better for him that a millstone were hanged around his neck, and he cast into the sea'" (Arendt 1973, p. 241 citing Luke 217:244). Arendt's esteem for speech, thought and action arises from her understanding of what contributes to healthy, happy and human existence. In order to identify from where these presumptions arise, I shall examine the qualities which establish thought as so virtuous. I shall then go on to use the example of Arendt's discussion of Adolf Eichmann to display how thought manifests itself through speech and action.

Central to Arendt's belief in the virtue of good communication is its ability to encourage thinking. Indeed, Arendt states that thought *is* a process of creating a dialogue with oneself—it is a highly personal, internal communication. The notion of thought as a conversation between "me" and "myself" has been central to philosophy since the time of Plato (Arendt 1958, p. 76). Arendt believes that such a dialogue creates an awareness of the nuances of existence by allowing an individual to internally relate the truths "in the world" such as facts, rules and disciplines to one's own "truths"— beliefs, experiences and feelings. The advantage of such a conversation with oneself is the inherent appeal of its honesty. A conversation between "me" and "myself" is unique in that both participants are communicating from the same position, within a shared understanding. Arendt refers to this "honesty" through evidence of a lack of external impetus. "Truth" she states, citing Thomas Aquinas, "can reveal itself only in complete human stillness" (Aquinas 1947, p. 182 cited in; Arendt 1958, p. 15), "thought...has neither an end nor aim outside of itself" (Arendt 1958, p. 170). Because it depends upon this internal communication, contemplative thought uncovers the honest admissions of the soul.

Arendt believes that the benefit of thinking is that it presents the ability to reflect upon basic human values. As Heidegger described it, "Thinking says what the truth of Being dictates; it is the original *dictare. Thinking* is primordial poetry" (Heidegger 1973-74, p. 583). We experience what we do while thinking because we are confronted in our own minds with what emerges from our "opaque and impenetrable" hearts (Arendt 1971, p. 418). The result of this inner contemplation is that it reveals the *truth*, not only about everything that can be held to be true in the phenomenal world, but also about the nature of the contemplator (Arendt 1958, pp. 75-76). Thought involves inherent critique from a position beyond reproach that is nonetheless subjectively constituted and unique. As Arendt notes in *The Life of the Mind*, "The experience of the activity of thought is probably the aboriginal source of our notion of spirituality in itself, regardless of the forms it has assumed" (Arendt 1978b, p. 44). Thought therefore stands as a model of ideal communication; as it is open, exploratory, reflective and seeks to reach an understanding.

The notion of spirituality provides us with an interesting way to distinguish the critical nature of thought and to understand the dichotomy Arendt establishes between "thinking" and "knowing". Thinking involves critical personal reflection; whereas knowing depends upon the acceptance of truth as *external to individual perception*. While Arendt believes that the process of prayer has much in common with the inner dialogue of thinking, there is a fundamental distinction as to whether critical space may emerge, which distinguishes thinking from knowing (Arendt 1958, pp. 76-77). Prayer may be likened to thought insofar as it involves a process of questioning dialogue, but the moment it becomes a process of passively beholding a "known" truth it ceases its relentless questioning and becomes "knowing". Knowing does not require the critical negotiation of the individual's perspective but rather requires the subjugation of the individual's will to what is known.

According to Arendt, modern times are distinguished by a propensity to "know" which arises from a deep mistrust of the human capacity to identify reality (Arendt 1958, p. 310). This reflects the themes of Immanuel Kant in his work "Answering the Question: What is the Enlightenment?", where he describes "the self incurred immaturity" of people who are afraid of independent thought (Kant 1985). While Kant's project rests upon supporting reason in the face of dogmatic religions and customs, Arendt suggests that modern "knowledge", as a flight from thought, also appears wherever we have unquestioning faith in something—scientific and economic rationality being two examples she uses of instances where we let our "knowing" override our "thinking".

The importance of this distinction between thinking and knowing can be seen in Arendt's encounter with the mind of Nazi war criminal Adolf Eichmann. Eichmann, previously a vacuum cleaner salesman, rose quietly through the managerial ranks of the Nazi party to be placed in charge of the Nazi's "final solution" to "the Jewish problem" during World War Two. This position entailed the design, construction and supervision of the Nazi death camps. When Eichmann was apprehended some years after the war Arendt attended the trials to report on them from a Jewish perspective. When confronted with Eichmann, the man who had planned the extermination of millions of human beings, what Arendt found remarkable was his banality; his evil nature existed not in the perverse nature of his thought, but in the lack of any critical thought and the subsequent dominance of external notions of truth.

For Arendt, what was lacking in Eichmann's thought process was the capacity to question the legitimacy of his own actions. He always did what he was told, he did his best to provide for his family and to be a success in the world in which he found himself. She did not see him as evil—he had no extraordinary characteristics at all, he was simply unable to challenge the beliefs of his superiors and his society with beliefs of his own—he simply did not *think* of what he was doing[1]. Arendt bases her estimation of Eichmann's thinking processes on both his speech and his action—his appearance in the world.

In support of this argument Arendt highlights the thoughtlessness of Eichmann's actions throughout his career in the Nazi Party. She asserts that Eichmann did not join the National Socialist party out of any deep-seated conviction, but rather as an unemployed and lonely individual who was looking for membership of any fraternity—indeed his application to the National Socialists was only submitted after he unsuccessfully attempted to join the Freemasons (Arendt 1964, p. 29). His rise through the ranks of the Nazi Party was not due to any particular brilliance on his part; his remarkable characteristics were rather that he was efficient and unquestioning. He distinguished himself by conceiving of a new way of processing disenfranchised Germans such as Jews and Gypsies, a sort of human *de-ssembly* line which would strip people of their citizenship, property and money in a series of detached and efficient procedures. Importantly, this sort of dehumanisation was successful due to its lack of contemplative involvement during the processing of people—no talking, no identities (captives were all tattooed with numbers) and no explanations. The death camps operated as a machine whose success was gauged upon its efficiency and the efficiency of the machine was heightened by specifically excluding contemplative human involvement. As an embodiment of this process, Eichmann distinguished himself by his capacity to act out the objectives set before him by the Nazi Party without question—as Arendt states he *"merely...never realised what he was doing"* (Arendt 1964, p. 288)[2].

Arendt's estimation of Eichmann's thoughtlessness is also based upon his qualities as a speaker. Arendt stresses that speech is the public manifestation of thought, insofar as "whatever men do or know or experience can make sense only to the extent that it can be spoken about" (Arendt 1958, p. 4). In this respect, Eichmann distinguished himself by his use of fixed expressions and reliance on unoriginal phrases that appeared to be a direct recital of party propaganda (Kristeva 2001a, p. 148). Arendt expressed dismay at his trite phrases and bureaucratic vernacular: "he was genuinely incapable of uttering a single sentence that was not a cliché" (Arendt 1964, p. 48). Arendt concludes from this that "his inability to speak was closely connected with an inability to think, namely, to think from the standpoint of somebody else" (Arendt 1964, p. 49). For Arendt, Eichmann's inability to speak without relying on clichés and fixed expressions exemplified the fact that his thinking also relied upon external templates, indicating that he did not think but, rather, knew.

Arendt's encounter with Adolf Eichmann illustrates why she believes a public sphere that fosters critical thought is so important. Without ever being encouraged to think about his actions and without ever having the opportunity to publicly debate the wisdom of his superiors, Eichmann found himself designing and commanding a machine responsible for the deaths of over five million people. He did so not because he was evil, but rather because he was well behaved in a society which did not foster freedom of thought, speech and action. Arendt is at pains to suggest that we ought to be aware that unless the contemporary realm of public communication encourages thoughtful engagement within our communities, we run the risk of producing nations of Eichmanns.

The Role of the Public Realm in Thought, Speech and Action

Arendt seeks to emphasise that the ciritical element in determining the health of a public realm is the action which that public realm facilitates. She uses labour, work and action as three different categories of activity through which to demonstrate the type of public realm manifested by each. She describes the public realm produced through the activity of labour as the public realm of *animal laborans*–or beasts of labour. The public realm produced through the activity of work is that of *homo faber*–or people of work. The public realm dominated by action is the only public realm for fully fledged humans (homo sapiens, or people of wisdom). Arendt's description of the public realms of labourers, workers and actors serves to reinforce how public communication can be seen to contribute to the formation of self and society.

Labour

In Arendt's conception, the public sphere of *animal laborans* is devoid of meaningful, expressive communication. Rather, the *animal laborans* is "imprisoned in the privacy of his own body, caught in the fulfilment of needs in which the body can share and which nobody can fully communicate" (Arendt 1958, pp. 118-119). The activity of labouring does not allow for thought, speech or (public) action and, as a result, does not manifest a community of people that arises out of speaking and acting together. Indeed, the labouring process is often designed to inhibit public contemplation, communication or action.

The activity of labour conditions the public actions made possible for labourers. If a person is trained to use their bodies to extract value for someone else's profit and if in the process they are taught that personal expression is wasteful, then they are unlikely to nurture their own capacities for thought, speech and action. Arendt's point is not that labourers are incapable of these faculties, but rather that any domain dominated by the activity of labour is unlikely to be critical because the capacity for thought, speech and action is discouraged. Slavery is not just the condition of not being able to decide one's own fate, slavery is enabled by the exclusion of slaves from public discussion.

Work

Homo faber distinguishes itself from *animal laborans* through its capacity for work. Work in turn distinguishes itself from labour through its tangible output; its reification in the material world. The danger of a public realm dominated by *homo faber* is that action is orchestrated through knowing, as opposed to thinking. Arendt's problem with this form of a public realm is intimately tied up with her fear of banality—of life without thought. This fear can be seen in a succinct description of the problem, which is worth quoting at length:

> The point of the matter is that Plato saw immediately that if one makes man the measure of all things for use, it is man the user and instrumentalizer, and not man the speaker and doer or man the thinker, to whom the world is being related. And since it is in the nature of man the user and instrumentalizer to look upon everything as a means to an end—upon every tree as potential wood—this must eventually mean that man becomes the measure not only of things whose existence depends upon him but of literally everything there is...If one permits the standards of *homo faber* to rule the finished world as they must necessarily rule the coming into being of this world, then *homo faber* will eventually help itself to everything and consider everything that is a mere means for himself. (Arendt 1958, p. 158)

Homo faber establishes utility as the known goal of action, and thereby reduces all action to work, and all debate to a discussion of means. While Arendt objects to the public realm of *animal laborans* due to its inability to manifest speech and action, her objection to the public realm of *homo faber* is based more on the type of consideration encouraged by such activity, which is knowing rather than thinking. As can be seen with Eichmann and the Nazis, the danger of a public realm dominated by knowing is that alternative values are never aired and one set of social presumptions becomes all-powerful.

Action

Arendt distinguishes action from work due to the fact that action has no predefined utility; it is generated by an actor and is entirely subjective and reflexive of the surrounds of the act. Action is "the only activity that goes on directly between men without the intermediary of things or matter" and, therefore "corresponds to the human condition of plurality [such as the plurality found in thought], to the fact that men, not Man, live on the earth and inhabit the world" (Arendt 1958, p. 7). Arendt presents action as subjective; that is not as instrumental but as iterative; not based in knowing but aware of plurality and, therefore, grounded in thought.

Action is distinguished from labour because, as Arendt explains, action is never silent but always exists as a manifestation of the person involved in the action. Here she follows the classical notion that through acting agents reveal something of their own nature (Dante 1950, p. 13). Action is an actualisation of the "who", a direct expression of the individual's unique existence that is both gratifying and ingratiating[3]. Unlike labour, which is silent and concerned only with sustaining life, action is a form of disclosure, and its prevalence gives rise to a very human conversation about the good.

In order to appreciate Arendt's vision of the virtue of an agonistic polis, it is helpful to realise that Arendt dismisses the public space of *animal laborans* and *homo faber* not because people in such realms *cannot* think, but rather because they *are not encouraged to do so.*

> The art of Politics teaches men to bring forth what is great and radiant, in the words of Democritus; as long as the polis is there to inspire men to dare the extraordinary, all things are safe; if it perishes, everything is lost…Greatness, therefore, or the specific meaning of each deed, can lie only in the performance itself and neither in its motivation nor its achievement. (Arendt 1958, p. 206)

The ideal public forum would provide everybody with "an opportunity to engage in those activities of expressing, discussing and deciding which in the positive sense are the activities of freedom" (Arendt 1990, p. 235). In opposition to the public realms of *animal laborans* and *homo faber*, Arendt places an idealised conception of the polis of Classical Greece. Deriving her perspective from the works of Plato and Aristotle, she imagines the polis as the ideal public space due to its ability to promote thought through providing a forum for action.

The Ideal Agonistic Polis

Arendt suggests that the closest approximation to a political public realm constituted by action occurred in the agora (public space) of Classical Athens. Unlike contemporary political forums, the Athenian polis was created to meet public needs and as a result no activity that served only the purpose of making a living was permitted to enter the political forum (Arendt 1958, p. 37). It was argued that to allow the public forum to be permeated by questions of economy would be contrary to its meaning. At the time economics was considered housekeeping, an essentially private matter that had no bearing on the debate on public virtue central to the function of the polis.

Instead, the function of the polis was to provide a forum for debate over virtue which would benefit the public by presenting a chance to win immortal fame. Through speech and action the polis of Ancient Greece provided a forum for citizens to express themselves in their unique distinctness, and gave them an opportunity to voice the story of their existence.

> The polis was permeated by a fiercely agonal spirit, where everybody had constantly to distinguish himself from all others, to show through unique deeds or achievements that he was best of all. The public realm, in other words, was reserved for individuality; it was the only place where men could show who they really and inexchangeably were. (Arendt 1958, p. 41)

Rather than being a forum for consensus, the polis provided an adversarial, yet not antagonistic, forum for revealing difference and justifying that difference as evidence of virtue through the telling of stories. This proliferation of stories was stimulated by public debate about what ought to be immortalised and by consideration of the good life; in turn the immediacy and intimacy of participation promoted thinking as opposed to knowing.

One reason Athenians wished to engage in the polis is because it is only in the light of public reception that identity can truly reveal itself. Arendt declares bluntly that "the essence of who somebody is cannot be reified by himself" (Arendt 1958, p. 211); rather someone's essence can only be grasped following their appearance before a relevant public (Arendt 1958, pp. 193-194). Who someone is remains hidden from the person in their private existence but appears in public "clearly and unmistakably to others" (Arendt 1958, p. 179). Identity may be a private attribute, developed through one's own thought and action, but publicity gives this identity meaning by gaining recognition in a truly plural forum. Arendt suggests that we seek to *realise* (literally—to make real) who we are through exposure to such a public.

The Athenian polis also provided a refuge against the transience of human life (Arendt 1958, p. 19). The polis, in institutionalising a communal forum for notions of the good life, provided some permanence to good actions that were communally admired—enabling great humans to leave a legacy for so long as that legacy maintained itself as a valid contribution. An eternally brilliant idea or act (such as Socrates' martyrdom or Pericles' speeches) would achieve eternal recognition in the polis of Classical Greece, as it would continue to guide and inform the lives of those involved in the polis. In turn the agent who conveyed this act would achieve the worthy goal of immortality.

By providing space that privileged action, the polis of Classical Greece harnessed the public spirit of the citizens in a forum that empowered individual uniqueness and encouraged adversarial debate. Arendt believes that these factors combined to produce a citizenry that was both critically informed and whose members were unafraid to assert their individuality[4].

The extent to which the public forum contributed to the citizen's sense of humanity can be seen when Aristotle describes slaves and barbarians as those deprived "of a way of life in which speech and only speech made sense and where the central concern of all citizens was to talk with each other" (Arendt 1958, p. 27). Where the central concern of the public realm is utility, we are condemned to an impoverished reality that has no public space for personal revelation and personal perspective.

The Problem with Modern Democracies

By claiming to "know" the legitimate way to distribute power, our representative democracies reduce their critical potential by *disengaging* with the public. This has the twofold effect of isolating the democratic system from public criticism and forcing individuals to express their individuality in less ideal and less public forums. Hannah Arendt's critique of modern democracies is often approached through her description of the occlusion of the political sphere by the social sphere[5]. Instead of a public space of plurality, we find a social space of behaviour[6]. The "social" is a catchall phrase to describe *homo faber's* and *animal laborans'* concurrent dominance of the public sphere. These values ensure that political participation is rationalised to mute tabulation of votes and political discussion is considered corrupt and impolite. With this in mind I intend to explore Arendt's discussion of the problem with the modern public realm through analysing her views on the growing dominance of instrumental thought which she perceives as the main obstacle to the establishment of an engaging and thought-provoking forum for speech and action.

The Philosophical Dominance of Instrumental Thought

If we were to question Arendt about an approximate time and place for a discernable origin of the problems of contemporary democracies, she would most likely point us towards the philosopher Descartes. Motivated by the discoveries of Galileo who, through the invention of the telescope, overthrew the popular belief of his time that the sun revolved around the earth, Descartes was the first to base his philosophical position upon a lack of faith in the adequacy of the human senses for revealing the world. Confronted with the evidence that even the most apparent truth could be factually incorrect, Descartes reduced his entire basis of knowledge to what he knew to be true, arriving at the obscure yet normatively significant statement "I think therefore I am". Descartes could not trust his eyes, his heart or his senses, he could only trust that he experienced the process of thinking; nevertheless, he did trust the telescope to tell him his senses could not be trusted! Arendt argues that Descartes' status as the first "modern" philosopher is attributable to his acceptance that the instrument of the telescope more readily interpreted reality than the faculties of his senses. He advanced the notion that reality was something that existed prior to our encounter with it and that reality could only be determined by removing the flaws created through human perception. This represents a philosophical privileging of knowing over thinking and has led to fundamental changes in the realms of thought, action and speech.

The assertion that truth was not to be arrived at through public thought, but rather through the manipulation of instruments can be seen as the origin of the philosophical ascendancy of *homo faber*. Prior to the invention of the telescope, truth had been the subject of philosophy—the most accurate account of reality was to be provided through a discussion between the various members of any community. These groups had arrived at the conclusion that the sun revolved around the earth and, as far as this understanding was coherent, it was true. Arendt argues that Galileo's use of the telescope did not render this truth invalid and indeed did not differ from the established arguments of many other philosophers without telescopes (Arendt 1958, p. 258). What changed the order of thought and knowledge was the acclaim given to the instrument itself, and Descartes' abdication before the evidence of the telescope as he concurrently reduced the realm of philosophy to accounting for the "experience between man and himself" (Arendt 1958, p. 254). Truth, from this point on, was to be determined through work rather than personal reflection. The instrument provided a demonstrable fact in place of speculation, and thus rendered all further speculation irrelevant. Science, through its process of measuring, naming and categorising, presented exciting new possibilities for human potential. At the same time, philosophy was shown to be subjective and obscure, and hence displaced from the role of imparting truth about the external world to that of commenting only on those aspects of existence that could not be objectively measured (Arendt 1958, pp. 303-304). From this point on, knowledge assumed a primacy over thought. Knowledge became oriented to how the universe affects our measuring instruments, a process that based itself on the reduction and elimination of human contemplation. Hence Descartes' assertion of the inadequacy of the senses to reveal truth limited the scope of philosophy at the same time as he reduced thinking to knowing.

This fundamental reversal of the hierarchy of thinking and knowing went hand in hand with the rise of *homo faber* in the realm of action. Following the instrumental turn of philosophy, the world of things inherited a new importance insofar as instruments could facilitate knowing. Arendt maintains that the break with thinking was consummated by the introduction of process into making (Arendt 1958, p. 301). Before this break, contemplation was considered an inherent element of making insofar as craftspeople were guided by their "idea" of what they wished to achieve, and retained the unique possibilities of action in the course of creation (Arendt 1958, pp. 301-302). Following this break, fabrication was better instructed through process, using tools, measurements and machinery to recreate a predefined "ideal". The ascendancy of knowing over thinking, and work over action, was evident in the introduction of instruction as the basis for fabrication, as opposed to contemplation and interpretation.

The ascendancy of the ideals of *homo faber* also has a deleterious effect upon the realm of speech. Despite the freedom of human agency and the eternal possibility of action, the instrumental nature of knowledge means that speech is only valued insofar as it might *command, instruct* or *resolve*. As we have seen, Arendt values speech for its power to *reveal* and, in doing so, inspire action. The fundamental difference here can once again be seen as being the elemental difference between thinking and knowing. The difference between action and work lies in their prioritisation of contemplation—in the act (in the case of thinking, acting and speaking) or external to, and in some sense prior to, the act (as in knowing, working and instructing). In witnessing the ascent of knowing, instructing and working over thought, speech and action Arendt suggests we can see the public realm of *homo faber* occluding the human public realm.

In investigating the relationship between the origins and subsequent problems of the modern political realm, it is easy to be too keen to suggest some kind of determinacy. It seems logical to believe that an uncritical public realm will generate uncritical citizens, which will in turn further reduce the critical capacity of the public realm in a never-ending downward spiral; and is it not equally true that a benign public sphere would be needed to be instrumentally applied to break this process? It is crucial to understand that determinacy of this sort is quite contrary to Arendt's faith in human agency— or our ability and our natural tendency towards expressive action (Arendt 1958, p. 236). The irrepressible agency of humanity, the possibility of action, is the source of all Arendt's hopes for an improved human condition.

A Format for an Ideal Agonistic Democracy

"The miracle that saves the world…from its normal, 'natural' ruin is ultimately the fact of natality" (Arendt 1958, p. 247). When something new comes into the world—be it a child or a political system—we are forced to consider the world into which it is brought. Arendt argues this forced contemplation is an irrepressible source of care for what is public. Through the continual creation of the new, we are reminded of the potency of action in a way that generates thought and speech. This irreducible aspect of humanity ensures that there shall always be some impetus towards democracy. In turn, Arendt suggests that democratic forums should be responsive to, and oriented towards, the direct participation of participants.

The personal and political benefits of participatory publics became apparent during the American Revolution, when local councils and militia constituted publics through their own activities and oratories. Arendt cites other examples of the awakening of political virtue, such as the French *societies revolutionaires*, the Russian soviets, the French Resistance, the Israeli kibbutzim and the American Civil Rights Movement. Each of these movements succeeded politically, as forms of resistance, because they sought to open up space for free public action (Isaac 1994, p. 163). As a result Arendt sees such council systems as "the single alternative that has ever appeared in history, and has reappeared time and time again" (Arendt 1972, p. 231). This continual appearance is evidence enough to Arendt that all that is required for a virtuous public realm is a place for people to speak and act about common concerns.

Arendt believes that the problem of ensuring that democratic polities remain meaningful for all participants can be solved through the dissemination of public space. As she wrote in *The Crises of the Republic*, "since the country is too big for us all to come together and determine our fate, we need a number of public spaces within it" (Arendt 1972, p. 232). In *On Revolution*, Arendt lauds a democratic system of tiered councils, each with its own internal deliberative mechanism, in which the members of each tier deliberatively elect their representative for the next highest council (Arendt 1990, p. 278). With this in mind, it is possible to understand the particular political virtue Arendt saw in Thomas Jefferson's ward system and in other theories and practices of revolutionary councils[7].

Thomas Jefferson's ward system was an attempt to harness the political capacities of public citizens through their involvement in small community "wards". He declared that a system of wards—polities roughly 24 square miles in size and each with their own school—would be "the most fundamental measure for securing good government, and for instilling the principles and exercise of good government into every fibre of every member of our commonwealth"[8]. Arendt argues that Jefferson perceives that the great danger to the United States republic is "that the constitution had given all power to the citizens, without giving them the opportunity of being republicans and acting as citizens" (Arendt 1990, p. 253). Arendt argues that Jefferson shares her understanding of the importance of personal involvement in politics:

> The basic assumption of the ward system, whether Jefferson knew it or not, was that no one could be called free without his experience in public freedom, and that no one could be called either happy or free without participating, and having a share, in public power. (Arendt 1990, p. 255)[9]

By making the domain of government that much smaller, along with giving each ward control of education, Jefferson advocates a polis that would demand the normative consideration of its citizens. Such a responsive polis would promote the benefits of political involvement; which is a boon to both the healthy function of the polis, and the healthy existence of the individual.

Arendt also makes the point in *On Revolution* that these exemplary publics are invariably constituted through the act of resistance to an illegitimate form of political power. People are forced to constitute their own public when they are confronted with a public existence they cannot reconcile with their private being. When people refuse to speak and act through the machinery of the state and instead choose to constitute their own forum, their own speech and their own action, by necessity they begin to constitute a new public realm. This public realm gains power simply because of its immediacy and responsiveness. Resisters "had become challengers, they had taken the initiative upon themselves, and therefore, without even noticing it, had begun to create the public space between themselves where freedom could appear" (Arendt 1968, pp. 3-4). In the act of resistance, people are forced to devise new structures of politics based upon their own notions of legitimacy, and in doing so are not only forced to think about the "stability and durability of the new structure" but also enjoy "the exhilarating awareness of the human capacity of beginning" (Arendt 1990, p. 223)[10]. Thus, the very act of creation is part of the experience offered by the ideal public realm.

Conclusion

Agonistic democrats can be understood to emphasise the importance of direct personal involvement in the communicative composition of power. To be truly free, their argument goes, the individual must have the opportunity to engage in the process of governance. Interestingly, agonistic theorists—such as Arendt and Mouffe—have made a number of equally important assertions. Firstly, the problems that contemporary democracies face are the result of the lack of this direct access. The lack of access results in the marginalisation of groups without a political voice; the marginalisation of participants leads to a lack of critical and diverse input into important decisions. Moreover, the predominance of invested, material interests which seek to instrumentalise the public sphere leads to an absence of a forum for individuals to express their identities, which in turn leads them to express themselves through wasteful materialism.

The accuracy of agonisitc views on modern democracy is readily apparent. Individuals do not feel like they are capable of expressing themselves in our democratic systems and politics is not considered polite conversation. Our formal mode of political expression—the vote—is typically reduced to what we believe is the most useful choice between two separate productive machines masquerading as political parties. Our public institutions equip us for knowing, learning and behaving; not for thinking, speaking and acting. Of course, the agonists are also remarkable for their utopian visions—direct democratic participation is not only difficult to facilitate in contemporary nations, it appears that citizens have neither the interest nor the inclination to undertake such participation. Agonists will argue that this lack of enthusiasm is a result of their impoverished experience of public life. In the latter part of this book we'll examine how agonism fares in the world of digital media, but first we'll turn our attention to a far more pragmatic version of ideal public communication—deliberative democracy.

Deliberative Democracy

> Majority rule, just as majority rule, is as foolish as its critics charge it with being. But it is never merely majority rule...the means by which a majority comes to be a majority is the more important thing.
>
> —John Dewey (1954)

With these words John Dewey outlines the spirit of deliberative democracy. Deliberative democrats base their ideal system not around participation but around the notion of an ideal process of democratic conversation. Whilst deliberative democrats share the agonists' desire to make the democratic process inclusive and flexible they argue they present a model of democratic interaction which is more suitable for the fractured publics of advanced economies. In the deliberative model the emphasis on personal involvement in politics is replaced by an emphasis on the correct procedure for public debate. Deliberative democrats tend to look at the problems and potential of communication on a personal level and then use those insights to critique public deliberation on a social level. In doing so, they focus on the procedures which govern communication.

In order to present the central elements of the deliberative democratic system, I shall focus on the work of Jurgen Habermas as the most prominent and prolific deliberative theorist. Habermas's *Theory of Communicative Action* introduces a set of concepts which can be used to understand the democratic potential of deliberation and the threats to this potential in modern societies. This chapter will initially explore Habermas's communicative theory and then go on to outline deliberative criticisms of modern democracy. Finally, the chapter details how deliberative democrats believe deliberation can be reformed to improve the quality of public discussion.

Answering the Question: What Is Communicative Action?[1]

The distinguishing feature of communicative action is that it is communication oriented to achieving understanding, as opposed to strategic action which is communication oriented to achieving results (Habermas 1984, p. 295)[2]. One way of understanding this dichotomy is by opposing communicative uses of communication to rhetorical uses of communication. While the study of rhetoric focuses on how communicative devices can be used to persuade and convince, the study of communicative action focuses on how communicative devices can be used to consider and understand. Habermas describes rhetorical forms of communication, such as advertising and election speeches, as "strategic action" as these forms involve using communication for strategic ends. On the other hand, forms of communication designed to increase understanding, rather than a predetermined goal, are considered to be "communicative action".

A communicative exchange is one where the outcome is determined by the cooperative search for "truth", the discussion ceases to be communicative if a preconceived notion of truth comes to dominate the discussion. Habermas suggests that communicative action makes up the majority of personal conversations. In such exchanges the actors seek to express themselves, reach an understanding about their situation, and to agree on a plan of action in order to coordinate their behaviour (Habermas 1984, pp. 85-86). When two parties reach an agreement on a particular issue they generally do so based upon the reasonableness of the various statements they have made, rather than submitting to a preconceived strategy. This allows the most readily justifiable and shared premises (what appears resasonable to all) to form the basis for agreement and action.

The earnest engagement of communicative action can be seen in contrast to strategic action where the statements of the speaker are designed to secure a strategic aim which is determined externally to the communicative process. During communicative action aims can be stated openly, but they are subject to change as agents maintain their fundamental ambition to achieve understanding by reorienting their own perspectives according to each other's validity claims (Brand 1990, p. 24). However, the aim of strategic action is not to achieve understanding, but to achieve a goal determined as desirable *prior* to the process of communication. Rather than having a commitment to achieving understanding, strategic actors have a commitment to a preconceived goal, and hence orient their validity claims around the successful achievement of that goal. In the case of strategic action, the act of communication is not undertaken in order to explore the possibilities of agreement, but rather in an effort to achieve a predetermined outcome.

The aim of communicative action is sustainable reasonable dialogue, but this dialogue ceases if strategic actors use discussion merely to pursue their preconceived strategic ends. The healthy development of communicative discussion is inhibited by the fact that strategic action is parasitic upon communicative exchanges, and the existence of a strategic actor in an exchange will prohibit the possibility of communicative action. For instance, if a group of friends is deciding what to do on the weekend and everyone is acting "communicatively" making statements about their interests and schedules, then just one actor (who has, for instance, already determined that they would like to go to the movies) can easily manipulate the group to that conclusion using strategic statements. The strategic actor can emphasise the reputation of the movie, can be deceitful about their other commitments on the weekend and can quietly ridicule the suggestions of others *all while appearing to be acting communicatively*. In fact, it is clear that the most successful strategic action is successful largely because it presents itself as communicative action.

The difference between communicative action and strategic action can thus be understood to reflect the difference Arendt posits between thinking and knowing; the former is oriented towards considering and understanding while the latter is oriented towards utilising and achieving. The difference between Habermas's communicative action and Arendt's conception of thinking is that Habermas understands communicative action to be a thoughtful *public* dialogue, whereas Arendt describes the same communicative process as an internal one. Achieving understanding in public situations is more challenging than achieving understanding through individual thought. There is a unity to the thinking processes of individuals that perseveres due to the "shared" experiences and norms of the person who undertakes the dialogue which is thought. The conversation that takes place between "me" and "myself" is one in which the experience and understandings of those conversing is identical. In order to replicate this unity, Habermas asserts there are certain conditions communicative actors must accept in order to achieve understanding. This form of "ideal speech" forms the basis of the procedural approach of deliberative democrats and shall be discussed at the end of this chapter. However, before we discuss the deliberative solution to democracy's problems, it's helpful to understand how the problem with democracies can be reconceived in the language of communicative action.

The Colonisation of the Lifeworld by the System

Habermas believes that expression and discussion are the primary roles of communication (Habermas 1984, p. 288). He suggests that the fundamental purpose of communication is to exchange information in order to cooperatively coordinate action. When this type of communicative exchange occurs regularly and naturally it generates the web of meaning that constitutes the *lifeworld*. The lifeworld can be understood, then, as the shared network of meaning that is the "correlate of the processes of reaching understanding" (Habermas 1984, p. 70). When communicative action occurs naturally, it occurs because the actors are coming to an understanding within the context of commonly shared and unproblematic background convictions—within a shared lifeworld. Within the lifeworld, communicative actors can orient their discussions around certain presuppositions that they take for granted, and these shared convictions provide the basis for a meaningful exchange. For instance, if I was to state "January is a great time for the beach"—people in the southern hemisphere would understand me as we share a lifeworld—that of people who enjoy summer in January. However if I was to make the same statement in the northern hemisphere, people would disagree with me because they share a different lifeworld—where August is a great time for the beach. Habermas argues that these background knowledges, convictions and unproblematic assumptions constitute our lifeworld. Sharing a lifeworld enables the possibility of communicative action and we can also use communicative action to expand our lifeworld (if we reasoned with each other we can all agree to say that "summer is a great time for the beach"!)[3]. Due to the self constituting nature of communicative action, the shared understandings of the lifeworld possess an inherent and indelible validity.

Habermas juxtaposes the communicative legitimacy of the lifeworld with the strategic legitimacy of the other major component of this worldview—the *system*. The system is composed of rational institutions whose goals are determined by the strategic functions of those institutions. While action coordination in the lifeworld is achieved through agreement based upon unproblematic and shared presuppositions, action coordination in the system tends to be coordinated through the use of money and power. The lifeworld is the correlate of actors pursuing communicative action; the system is the correlate of actors pursuing strategic action.

Habermas argues that the colonisation of the lifeworld was enabled by the failure of mythical world views to sustain their coherence against the rise of science—a process he describes as the "rationalisation of the lifeworld". The resulting loss of shared beliefs, combined with the rise of instrumentalism, enabled the development of many different social subsystems; family, work, government, church and so on. Each subsystem has their own set of beliefs and values which enable them to function towards their particular goals. In the place of one overarching system of belief—religion—which dominated the beliefs and values of government, family and work, each of these different institutions began to organise themselves according to their own goals.

Whereas once everything was organised according to the "word of god", now governments are judged on their ability to provide prosperity and security, not their ability to maintain the world the way god intended.

In Habermas's analysis, these subsystems have become somewhat detached from the legitimising power of the lifeworld, yet continue to command authority due to their internal legitimacy. For instance, many parents are generally confused when asked by their children "why do you have to go to work all the time?" There is no easy way to explain this to a child, as the child has not been exposed to the systems involved: you can try "we need the money" which will invariably receive the question "why?", "so we may eat"; in which case the child may ask "but can't we grow food?" Inevitably such questions unveil complex systems of beliefs and values which aren't readily explainable to children but are readily apparent to those who are engaged in social systems. "I need to work because we want to be prosperous enough to enable you to have enough opportunity to learn the immense amount of knowledge which you will need to survive in an increasingly complicated future." Children of a non-colonised lifeworld will have a hard time understanding this: "But can't we just have fun?"

The prevalence of systemic rationalities in domains of cultural reproduction (such as public space, mass media and the education system) causes systemic imperatives to pervade the rationality of the lifeworld. This "colonisation" distorts the inherent reason of the lifeworld and undermines the critical function of individuals within democratic institutions—it limits their capacity to think, speak and act.

In order to gain an appreciation of the ways in which the system can begin to encroach upon the lifeworld, it is important to understand how systemic imperatives are accepted by the lifeworld. In archaic societies action was coordinated through a basic normative agreement that transcended "domains of rationality", such as cognition, morality and aesthetics. Following the rationalisation of the lifeworld, however, there is no universal normative consensus through which the coordination of action can be assured. The undermining of consensus occurs concurrently with new possibilities of individualisation; namely the ability of individuals to develop a subjective and differentiated attitude with regard to the realms of cognition, morality and aesthetics. Due to this individuation, the integration of society becomes absurdly complex and, indeed, in Habermas's view, impossible to orchestrate through universal agreement.

Thus, when systemic subsystems seek to coordinate action, each subsystem is typically unable to do so solely through communication. Systemic action must be coordinated, therefore, through "steering media" such as money and power. Thus

> ...in the wake of capitalist modernization money and power—more concretely, markets and administrations—take over the integrative functions which were formerly fulfilled by consensual values and norms, or even by processes of reaching understanding. (Habermas 1993, p. 171)

Money and power serve the role of steering media because their distribution can allow for the mediation of disputes over action without having to achieve agreement through communication. Quite simply, normative disagreement within and between subsystems is compensated by the distribution of money or power. So we find in the system that money and power provide the incentive for action rather than the inherent coordinating power of communicative consensus in the lifeworld. Rather than resort to the clumsy and possibly action-inhibitive mechanism of reaching consensus on shared issues, the use of "steering media" buys out disagreement and allows for the smooth functioning of systemic operation ("So you don't want to paint my fence? How about I pay you to do it?"). Given these terms, it is now possible to recast the problem with modern democracies as a result of the gradual replacement of communicative forms of action coordination with strategic forms of action coordination.

The Problem with Modern Democracies

According to Habermas, the problems of modernity occur because systemic power is, in the modern and postmodern era, progressively usurping the consensual communicative basis for the coordination of action. "The transfer of action coordination from ordinary language to steering media has the effect of uncoupling interaction from lifeworld contexts" (Habermas 1987b, p. 263). Given the inherent vulnerability of communicative action to strategic action, the colonisation of the lifeworld can be seen as the inevitable result of the effect of "steering media" on situations of action coordination. The ability to alter norms and values within the lifeworld is disproportionately possessed by those who have money and power.

The rather clumsy term "steering media" is employed by Habermas to illustrate that those who control money and power also control the steering capacity within any given society. For instance, in modern liberal democracies the institutions of property and contract govern the flow of money, while power is largely governed via the public-legal organisation of offices (Habermas 1987b, p. 270). Due to the universal, non-communicative nature of steering media, those who hold a superior position in the distribution of money and power have a greater opportunity to implement their strategic goals without having to secure a consensus. Furthermore, as the lifeworld shrinks to become one subsystem among many, it becomes susceptible to the possibility that its legitimacy is not as immediate and recognisable as that of other subsystems.

This situation is exacerbated by the fact that strategic acts are parasitic upon communicative acts. The moment strategic aims are introduced into an exchange, communicative action ceases, and the linguistic exchange becomes corrupted. However, if those acting communicatively are unaware of the presence of a strategic actor they typically adjust their positions to accommodate the strategic actor. We are presented, therefore, with a situation in which the ongoing reproduction of the lifeworld is susceptible to external and instrumental interference. When systemic forces achieve positions of control and distribution in regard to steering media, this can lead, either overtly or indirectly, to the infiltration of strategic voices into previously communicative exchanges.

> It is not the uncoupling of media-steered subsystems and of their organizational forms from the lifeworld that leads to one-sided rationalization or reification of everyday communicative practice, but only the penetration of forms of economic and administrative rationality into areas of action that resist being converted over to the media of money and power because they are specialized in cultural transmission, social integration and child rearing, and remain dependent on mutual understanding as a mechanism for coordinating action. (Habermas 1987b, p. 330)

As systemic knowledge permeates previously inaccessible realms of human conduct, we open ourselves up to greater levels of systemic colonisation through socialisation. The structurally differentiated and systemically colonised lifeworld, upon which modern states are fundamentally dependent, remains the only source of legitimation (Habermas 1987b, p. 359). The fact that language functions not only as a medium of reaching understanding, but also of socialisation and social integration in the process of identity formation (Habermas 1987b, p. 24) means that, in the process of socialisation, systemic imperatives have an opportunity to pervade, or colonise, the lifeworld.

Public education is a relatively benign example of this occurrence, and a comparison of the public education system of Ancient Athens, with the public education system of the Enlightenment, as depicted by Charles Dickens in *Hard Times*, can be very helpful in identifying the ways in which education developed (as a result of systemic imperatives) to be less about thinking, and more about knowing. The Athenian mode of education was focused on what might be called human development; that is, developing all human capacities including honing aesthetic, athletic and mental abilities. The purpose of these activities was to enable reflection upon one's life; to "know thyself", and in doing so, encourage understanding. The education of modernity, however, as articulated by Dickens' character Principal Gradgrind in *Hard Times*, is based upon reverence for facts and quantifiability. These skills provide the tools through which it is possible to become a useful member of an independent subsystem, but their centrality to education means that certain systemic presuppositions actually become presuppositions of the *lifeworld*. Under Gradgrind's supervision, the individual is not expected to develop as a human but as a worker; as a potential tool in a functional subsystem. In such ways, as forms of administrative and economic rationality penetrate into areas that, in effect, set social agendas, the lifeworld opens itself up to systemic colonisation.

What Habermas objects to in this process of lifeworld colonisation is essentially the same kind of cultural domination that Herbert Marcuse protests against in *One Dimensional Man* and Arendt criticises in *The Human Condition*. The criticism is that in advanced liberal democracies the voices of considered and human reason are being drowned out by the rationality of strategically oriented subsystems (Habermas 1992, p. 444). What Habermas objects to is

> the degree of autonomy that has been achieved by more or less automated social subsystems that, in the interest of efficiency, remove all sorts of policies from the sphere of public discussion where they could be assessed in the light of the desirability of the outcomes they actually produce (Olafson 1990, p. 65).

The colonisation of the lifeworld describes the situation wherein these subsystems secure their freedom from lifeworld legitimacy and determine success according to their own strategic criteria. In doing so, the subsystems undermine the very possibility of critical discussion about their outcomes.

In summary the theory of communicative action is underpinned by two basic notions. The first is that there are several different forms of speech that can be employed in communication. The two forms of action critical to our understanding of Habermas's democratic theory are strategic action, which can be defined as action oriented towards realising goals, and communicative action, through which actors seek to reach an understanding in order to agree on how to coordinate their action (Habermas 1984, pp. 85-86). The second idea underpinning communicative action is that there is a distinction between system and lifeworld; the lifeworld is the realm of personal relationships and is constituted by communicative action, while the system integrates society through functional or cybernetic feedback and is ordered on the basis of non-linguistic steering media, such as money and power (Calhoun 1992, p. 30; Habermas 1987b, p. 152). These concepts provide the basis for Habermas's deliberative democratic theory.

Ideal Speech: The Importance of Being Earnest

Deliberative democrats suggest that the solution to the problem of the increasing influence of money and power within democracies lies in developing standards for correct procedures in all decision making forums. Through ensuring that all decisions are judged against the accepted truths of the lifeworld, and not those perpetrated by the system, it is possible that earnest discussion can undermine the undue influence of those with money and power. Rather than attempt to design one political system to suit every situation, deliberative democrats have concentrated on developing a set of procedures which are based around the democratic rights of the individual. As with agonists, deliberative democrats tend to shy away from being overly prescriptive in identifying a specific concrete democratic structure that would serve equally well for all purposes. Rather, they use deliberation as an ideal against which to criticise actually existing democratic structures. Habermas is particularly helpful in this respect as he has several ideas as to how ideal speech might proliferate through existing democratic mechanisms such as state institutions and common law. What follows is an exploration of Habermas's deliberative solution to the problem with modern liberal democracies.

The Ideal Speech Situation

In order to produce the greatest degree of communicative action during decision making processes, Habermas describes an "ideal speech situation" to which all such conversations should aspire. Habermas presents this idealisation in order to point out the fundamental principles of democratic legitimacy. Through pursuing a number of discursive conditions designed to heighten understanding, Habermas argues that it is possible to limit the effect of money and power upon decision making processes.

The first specification Habermas makes about the ideal speech situation relates to who should contribute to the dialogue. The principle of participation can be best summarised by stating that everyone affected by the decision should be free to speak, and to speak freely (Habermas 1990, p. 86). This principle emphasises the liberal nature of Habermas's ideal forum. The extension of the forum to all parties affected not only rests upon the notions of freedom and equal rights but also echoes John Stuart Mill's passion for the inclusion of marginalised voices in order to achieve the most well-informed debate possible. Habermas emphasises that the broader the consideration that any decision undergoes, the more legitimate the outcome is likely to be (Rehg & Bohman 2002, p. 46).

In order to establish a discussion in which communicative action would flourish, Habermas depicts a situation in which care and understanding tend to develop between participants. For instance, in an early piece "A Theory of Communicative Competence", he suggests that the condition of ideal speech relies upon the ability of the ego to assume the subjectivity of alter ego and vice versa; a condition he calls "intersubjectivity". He argues that this takes place when there is complete symmetry among participants in a conversation.

> Pure intersubjectivity exists only when there is complete symmetry in the distribution of assertion and dispute, revelation and concealment, prescription and conformity among the partners of communication. (Habermas 1970, p. 371)

Symmetry among participants would mean that the notion of shared purpose would eliminate the instrumental uses of strategic discourse (rhetoric), and thus encourage the proliferation of earnest discussion. Such a discussion would result in communicative action; in which case the most rational, acceptable, action coordination would result.

In speech situations that cannot be fully symmetrical[4], Habermas argues that certain commitments be undertaken by participants in order to emulate the condition of pure intersubjectivity. Fundamentally, the participants need to be committed to reaching an understanding, rather than reaching a predetermined goal. To this end, the communicative process should exclude all force except the force of the better argument, and should exclude all motives but the cooperative search for the "truth". "From this perspective argumentation can be *conceived as a reflexive continuation, with different means, of action oriented to reaching understanding*" (Habermas 1984, p. 25). As persuasive rhetoric will fundamentally undermine the reasonable quality of conversation produced by this process, the sole goal of participants in conversation needs to be reaching understanding—not persuading.

In order to ensure that this understanding is achievable in non-symmetrical conditions, participants must be willing to rephrase their own arguments in a way that all participants can understand. Claims about truth and rightness must be redeemed so that they are understood by all participants (Habermas 1993, p. 171). In order to ensure that the debate takes shape based upon terms that are understood by all concerned parties, participants "should ascribe identical meanings to expressions and connect utterances with context-transcending validity claims" (Habermas 1996, p. 4). Essentially, participants must endeavour to explain themselves in a way that can be understood by all. Such a process leads to each participant gaining a more intimate knowledge of the arguments, the speakers, and the communication community of which they are part, which, in the process, facilitates and encourages action coordination based upon understanding.

The ideal speech situation is one in which all participants have the same understanding of language and seek the same goals. In typical situations where this symmetry does not exist, the single goal of communicators must be to achieve understanding. In order to achieve this goal, they must be prepared to explain and examine their language and arguments in such a way as to make them intelligible to all other participants—and they should be prepared to change and negotiate their own position in an effort to achieve understanding. Such a process gives rise to the most reasonable results in decision making situations.

Domains of Application

So how can these idealisations be implemented in a way that might improve democratic systems? This is the question Habermas seeks to address in his later work on democracy, most notably in *Between Facts and Norms* (Habermas 1996). The practice of deliberative democracy can be seen to open up administrative forums and domains of power to public scrutiny. Through public interrogation of rhetoric it is possible to highlight and undermine the public steering capacity of money and power.

Deliberative democracy presents a model of democratic decision making that ideally should proliferate through legal institutions, political institutions and the public sphere (Cooke 1997, p. 274). In *Between Facts and Norms*, Habermas presents the legal system as an example of the institutionalisation of those speech conditions he had come to realise as ideal. Habermas argues that courts of law act as a forum for allowing the voices of the lifeworld to compete against systemic forces in relatively ideal conditions. Working as an autonomous subsystem, law "translates ordinary language into specialized codes, regenerates social solidarity through universal(ized) norms, and institutionalizes radical democracy as equal rights" (Love 2002, p. 321). However, because the validity of the courts relies directly upon the support of the communicative community, their value lies in their ability to coordinate actions through legitimacy constituted through ideal speech (Habermas 1996, p. 462). With their specific rules about revelation, language and deliberation, the law courts of modern democracies represent an attempt to institutionalise the ideal speech situation. It is only in a court of law that participants in discourse are under an oath to speak honestly, openly and redeem any claims to truth that they make. Habermas argues that courts of law are constituted through the need for communication communities to emulate ideal speech so that the conditions of common life might be regulated impartially (Habermas 1996, p. 306).

Insofar as law courts present the opportunity to oppose the public influence of money and power through recourse to what is commonly held to be legitimate, it follows that Habermas identifies positive law as an already constituted means to allow deliberative access to issues of public importance. An example of this can be found in the "McLibel" case, where a concerned couple mounted a legal challenge against McDonald's advertising for targeting children and for portraying their food as nutritious[5]. By making McDonald's redeem their claims to truth in a court of law, it was publicly shown that such claims were illegitimate, and hence allowed citizens to exercise some control over the world in which they lived.

However, before we conclude that the rule of law ensures personal sovereignty, Habermas points out that the validity of the rule of law can only be established in the context of a vibrant and discursive political public sphere (Habermas 1996, p. xlii). The point he makes is that without a vibrant and healthy public sphere, a jury or a judge is unlikely to be a source of valid norms. This is an outgrowth of the problems posed by the systemic colonisation of the lifeworld. If the lifeworld itself has been colonised, then the judicial system will not be based upon a communicatively constituted lifeworld, but rather upon the systemic imperatives that have managed to infiltrate the lifeworld through processes of socialisation. Hence, law cannot operate independently in controlling the colonisation of the lifeworld by the system; it also requires a discursive public sphere in order to maintain the internal legitimacy of the lifeworld.

According to Habermas, the way to fix democracy is to implement discursive procedures that promote ideal speech both in the political realm and concurrently in the informal processes of communication in the public sphere (Habermas 1996, p. 376). For a democracy to claim legitimacy, therefore, both the political apparatus and civil society must be imbued with a discursive spirit which ensures that all public affairs are open to deliberation.

Habermas and his fellow deliberative democrats hope that the development of discursive ethics, as a self-reflexive search for understanding and reconciliation of identity with environment, will give rise to a critical civil society, which will in turn generate a legitimate democracy. In order to meet Habermas's requirements of legitimate democracy, a vibrant public sphere must "not only detect and identify problems but also convincingly and influentially thematize them, furnish them with possible solutions, and dramatize them in such a way that they are taken up and dealt with by the parliamentary complex" (Habermas 1996, p. 359).

William Rehg and James Bohman have pointed out that Habermas presents four functional requirements for a democratic public sphere that elaborate on this statement (Rehg & Bohman 2002). First, the public sphere must be receptive to the problems of citizens in their everyday lives. Second, it must be rooted in robust civil society and an open, pluralist culture to ensure that problems are brought to the attention of the public. Third, the public sphere should act as a unifying conduit between different segments of civil society in order to ensure inclusivity and broad debate. Fourth, the public sphere should be free of communicative blockages or distortions so that the public sphere can place issues on the political agenda without being controlled or distorted by powerful social interests (Rehg & Bohman 2002, pp. 41–42). The first two conditions deal with detecting and identifying issues of real importance to the community. The second two conditions reflect the requirements of a public sphere which can thematise and dramatise problems so that they are dealt with publicly and reasonably by the political apparatus. Deliberative democrats believe that the existence of this kind of public sphere would facilitate the critical consideration of political action and critical access to the political system.

Habermas believes that liberal democratic systems tend to meet the first three of these conditions, but he is critical of the role of the mass media in achieving the fourth condition. The media clearly play a central role in the functioning of the public sphere and, according to his discourse ethics, Habermas advances a series of requirements the media should satisfy if they are to fulfil their role as public communicators. He does this using the work of Michael Gurevitch and Jay G. Blumler, who identify the following services that the media ought to provide in democratic political systems:

1. Surveillance of the sociopolitical environment, reporting developments likely to impinge, positively or negatively, on the welfare of citizens;

2. Meaningful agenda-setting, identifying the key issues of the day, including the forces that have formed and may resolve them;

3. Platforms for an intelligible and illuminating advocacy by politicians and spokespersons of other causes and interest groups;

4. Dialogue across a diverse range of views, as well as between powerholders (actual and prospective) and mass publics;

5. Mechanisms for holding officials to account for how they have exercised power;

6. Incentives for citizens to learn, choose and become involved, rather than merely to follow and kibitz over the political process;

7. A principled resistance to the efforts of forces outside the media to subvert their independence, integrity and ability to serve the audience;

8. A sense of respect for the audience member, as potentially concerned and able to make sense of his or her political environment. (Gurevitch & Blumler 1990, p. 270)

These measures are designed to ensure that public issues are brought to public attention and that discussion of these issues is free from the distortion of systemic influences, thus reflecting the principles of ideal speech. It is clear that Habermas hopes that an effective media might force public communicators to be more communicative and less strategic, so that public actors might pre-emptively redeem their claims to truth and present arguments in broadly understandable language.

Conclusion

Habermas's work gives us scant indication as to how the civil society required to generate democracy's critical capacities might come about, but we have an eloquent metatheoretical conception of how democratic legitimacy should be constituted. The great simplicity of Habermas's theory is that it relies upon the rationality inherent in everyday communication. This communication is responsible for the reproduction of the lifeworld, and this is where social norms have the greatest communicative interaction with systemic forces. In the public sphere Habermas asserts that "the formation of rational opinions and decisions must rest on validity claims to truth, rightness and so forth, which can or at least could be justified before all competent persons with convincing reasons"[6]. In both private and public scenarios the key to Habermas's answer to the problem with modern democracies lies in appropriating the correct democratic *procedure*. The strength of his argument lies in his elegant and exhaustive exploration of what is required to make democratic procedures inherently legitimate.

> By singling out a procedure of decision making, it seeks to make room for those involved, who must then find answers on their own to the moral-practical issues that come at them, or are imposed upon them, with objective historical force. (Habermas 1990, p. 211)

Communicative action gives us a form of public deliberation that is both culturally sensitive and immanently critical. Asking for claims to truth to be redeemed is both a reasonable and critical expectation that opens up the possibility for democratic interactions.

We can see, then, that according to Habermas the emancipatory potential of democracy essentially rests upon his understanding that power is communicatively generated and that sovereignty can be seen as resting in critical access to public communication. According to Habermas, in order to fully cater to contemporary notions of sovereignty, democratic institutions need to become more open, deliberative and inclusive. At the same time, he believes all institutions should aspire towards becoming more democratic. The ideal speech of communicative action provides an exemplar for all reasonable discussions to emulate, and as such serves as an emancipatory mechanism for reforming systemic institutions.

CHAPTER THREE

Media, Technology and Democracy

Burn down the disco
Hang the blessed DJ
Because the music that they constantly play
It says nothing to me about my life

—The Smiths, 'Panic' (1986)

According to pop music folklore, the song lyric above was inspired when a BBC Radio DJ followed up a news report announcing the nuclear meltdown at Chernobyl with the sexy and cheerful single 'I'm Your Man' by *Wham!*. As such, it serves as an introduction to the notion that the mass media does not necessarily improve the quality of public communication. While Habermas and Arendt suggest that democracy's success depends upon the involvement of heroic individuals and conscientious processes in political issues, there's little evidence that the contemporary public sphere generates either of these elements. The aim of this chapter is to identify the role mass media plays in the discussions of modern democracies. It is important to understand the role that media technology has played in transforming what we conceive to be the public and how that transformation has changed our relationship with the public.

The ideal notion of the function of the media within representative democracy was evident in Thomas Carlyle's description of the French media at the time of the revolution as the "Fourth Estate" of government. The first estate being the clergy, the second the nobility and the third being the representatives of the people in the Estates General, it fell to the journalists, or the "Fourth Estate", to provide a medium between the Estates General and the common people. Carlyle portrayed the media here as heroes—opening up the corridors of power to public scrutiny and involvement—an extension to, and integral part of, a democratic system. However, his representation of the fourth estate also alludes to journalists as power holders—even in the old Estates General, the role of the editors and publishers in representing public affairs was integral to the success of a political enterprise. As such, less than 50 years after Carlyle described the press so valiantly, Oscar Wilde was declaring "at the present moment [the press] is the only estate. It has eaten up the other three. The Lords Temporal say nothing, the Lords Spiritual have nothing to say, and the House of Commons has nothing to say and says it. We are dominated by Journalism" (Wilde 2005, p. 255).

Examples of the media's failure to act as a conduit for public communication abound in day-to-day life; one of the clearest examples from the early 21st century being the "September dossier" of 2002 which contained information based upon sensationalised media reports and subsequently used as the basis for the invasion of Iraq. The information contained in this dossier—which suggested that Saddam Hussein had an active and capable Weapons of Mass Destruction Program—was used by the British Prime Minister Tony Blair as justification for military intervention and widely disseminated by the media in the lead up to the war on Iraq. While the allegations in the September dossier were influential in swinging public and political support towards an armed invasion of Iraq, in time it was revealed that these allegations were completely false (CIA 2004). Instead of operating as some kind of watchdog for the weak, in this instance the media proved to be a mouthpiece for the powerful. The September dossier showed up some of the inherent structural flaws of a public sphere facilitated through mass media. On one hand, commercial media had sought to establish the Iraq situation as more dire and distressing than it really was—in order to sell more news. Tony Blair then gave an air of authority to sensational media by presenting the dossier as legitimate research, which he was able to do because of the lack of critical scrutiny of his actions in parliament. Finally, the media went on to sensationalise the statements Blair subsequently made about Weapons of Mass Destruction precisely because the information had so much impact. The relationship between media and politics which is suggested by such an example is one of complicity. The goal of each system has become directed towards the stability and growth of the system itself. Politicians seek to become re-elected and journalists seek to sell more stories—no one needs argue with this situation unless we have a normative understanding that journalists or politicians have some kind of public duty. And according to agonistic theorists, we are increasingly distanced from feeling part of any kind of public life. What follows is a description of how media has developed from Thomas Carlyle's notion of the "Fourth Estate" to a part of the problem with contemporary democracies.

The Structural Transformation of the Public Sphere

In his work *The Structural Transformation of the Public Sphere*, Habermas sets out to identify how the public sphere has changed over the past two hundred years. Habermas, along with Carlyle, suggests that the ideal form of public space—one that was both critical and empowered—existed for a transient moment in representative democracies before being undermined by concurrent changes in state and media interference in the public realm. Habermas's ideal public sphere "cannot be abstracted from the unique developmental history of that 'civil society' from which it emerged" (Habermas 1989, p. xvii). In order to gain a thorough appreciation of the qualities of the ideal public sphere, and its subsequent transformation and decline, I shall delineate three historical epochs of publicity. The first is the feudal public sphere, characterised by "representative publicity". The second is the bourgeois public sphere, characterised by informed and reasonable public debate. The third is the modern public sphere, where the contradictions of the bourgeois public sphere manifest themselves through the replacement of critical debate with antagonistic representation. Each of these epochs shall be examined in turn in order to illustrate the rise and fall of the critical public sphere.

The Feudal Public Sphere

The feudal public sphere distinguished itself by its exclusivity. Using the courts and halls of medieval Europe as the template for the public life of the time, Habermas argues that in the Middle Ages access to a public forum was a consequence of status, not an innate human right (Habermas 1989, p. 7). Those who maintained public stations did so in a representative capacity, as an embodiment of some sort of "higher" power, commensurate with the status of divinity at the time. "The feudal powers, the Church, the prince and the nobility" were the public bearers of authority and maintained a "divine right" to rule (Habermas 1989, p. 11). These public figures served to represent virtue to the masses; to embody, and to some extent enact, the higher aspirations of the larger population.

An important part of maintaining the authority of such divine rulers was excluding access to the general public. Only through maintaining the appearance of exclusive divinity could the concentration of power appear legitimate. Therefore the public realm of the feudal epoch rested precisely upon the lack of critical public interaction. Publicity was wedded to the staging of events, in which personal attributes, such as insignia, dress and demeanour, were the important elements of a successful appearance (Habermas 1989, p. 8). These attributes brought acclaim and allegiance from the masses because, in effect, they were employed for their awe and adulation[1]. The means of education were controlled in this situation by the same authorities that maintained the tradition of exclusion, and this ensured a certain continuity of tradition. Reading and literary production took place more as forms of conspicuous consumption by those holding office rather than as a serious critical engagement (Habermas 1989, p. 38).The small amount of public communicative media—for the most part religious texts and congregations—were dominated by display and allegory, rather than action and reason. As can be seen in the transplantation of European monarchies throughout the Middle Ages, even "cataclysmic" political change manifested itself through the exchanging of symbols and personal attributes rather than through public communication[2]. The feudal public sphere distinguished itself as being both exclusive and non-critical.

According to Habermas, the eventual decline of the feudal public sphere was brought about by the rise of the printing press and the subsequent expansion of critical-rational discussion. This discussion, in turn, had been stimulated by the concurrent development of trade in both goods and news. As trade routes developed and market-driven calculations depended more and more upon foreign circumstances, so did the necessity of exchanging information about more distant events (Habermas 1989, p. 16). The mounting traffic of news concerning the increasing numbers of foreign lands led quite naturally to a more varied and critical discussion of what up until this time had been considered beyond reproach. The strata of society whose profits depended upon trade found it increasingly beneficial not only to know about foreign affairs, but also to understand the ramifications of certain events. As a consequence rational-critical debate began to proliferate in the coffee houses and salons of the trading centres of Europe (Habermas 1989, pp. 20-44). The rise of capitalism and the emergence of a mercantile trading class can therefore be seen as fundamental to the erosion of the feudal public sphere. It's particularly interesting that the increasing desire on behalf of elites to encounter difference led to the expanding trade routes that in turn contributed to the sharing of news and ideas which resulted in the decline of the feudal era. In Habermas's opinion it was this proliferation of communication and increasing levels of exchange and social complexity that formed the basis of the subsequent rational challenge to these same elites' appropriation of public power.

The new mercantilist bourgeoisie, empowered by critical discussion, began to place pressure on the public elites for political changes that would allow a greater share of wealth and power. What united this emerging class was that as a whole it was excluded from political participation; its members shared a common interest due to their equal exclusion, and also shared a common forum for dissent in civil society (Habermas 1989, p. 35). Due to its exclusion from state power, and its increasing self-awareness of its own critical-rational abilities, the bourgeois civil society that emerged excelled at promoting critical engagement. Fuelled by the fervour ignited through both the power of critical engagement and the denial of a state forum for this engagement, coffee houses and salons became hotbeds of political discussion. Also, as exemplified by the role of the works of Thomas Paine and John Locke in inspiring the American Revolution, the reading of critical works fostered public engagement. While Habermas undoubtedly admires the critical fervour of the bourgeois media, he also emphasises that the political will of the class was triggered by frustration with the structural limitations of the feudal public sphere.

The Bourgeois Public Sphere

The distinguishing feature of the bourgeois public sphere was that it was founded upon the grounds of reason—not upon a mythic claim to leadership but rather on a claim to rights which appeared self-evident. The movement away from myth and tradition as a basis for social organisation can be seen in Kant's essay "Answering the Question: What is Enlightenment?" (Kant 1985). Here Kant argues that enlightenment, "man's emergence from his self-incurred immaturity", depends upon public freedom and, more crucially, "the public use of reason" (Kant 1985, pp. 54–55). Kant held that as long as a society was open enough to publicly debate its rules and procedures, "the public sphere" could form the basis of the political-legal order and, at the same time, foster enlightenment (Habermas 1989, p. 104). Enlightenment discourses such as Kant's highlighted the irrational injustices of the feudal political system and the utopian possibilities of political freedom. The growth of the general reading public, the emergence of a bourgeois class that coveted political power, and the increased faith in the power of reason and science all contributed to the eventual downfall of the feudal public sphere.

The rise of the bourgeois public sphere occurred concurrently with a rise in the belief in the ability of society to politically organise itself through rational debate. Political writers such as Thomas Paine, Voltaire and Jean-Jacques Rousseau were challenging the validity of divine rule and increasingly using rational arguments as a basis for political organisation. The US Declaration of Independence is possibly the most famous instance of trying to describe this new form of legitimacy. The framers of the declaration based their claims for independence primarily upon what was universal and reasonable, famously stating:

> We hold these truths to be self-evident, that all men are created equal, that they are endowed by their Creator with certain unalienable Rights, that among these are Life, Liberty and the pursuit of Happiness.—That to secure these rights, Governments are instituted among Men, deriving their just powers from the consent of the governed. (*The U.S Declaration of Independence*, 1776)

The declaration goes on to list a series of reasons for the illegitimacy of English rule and reasons justifying US independence. The suggestion that public reason—not divine right—is the rightful basis of social organisation retains some of its vitality to this day and provides a testament to the brilliance of the bourgeois public sphere.

The institutionalisation of the bourgeois public sphere involved establishing the forum of bourgeois debate at a political level. Into the constitutions of the new democracies went safeguards for the freedom of communication and assembly, a division between executive and legislative power and an extension of the franchise to involve more "critical" voices. The impetus for freedom of communication and the right of assembly arose from the spirit of enlightenment, and the fresh memories of the political submission of the bourgeoisie. The division between legislative and executive powers served to institute a degree of critical reflection in the process of public debate. And the extension of the franchise to include all property owners ensured a political public that was constituted by educated and critical citizens (Habermas 1989, pp. 71–85). Politics was to be conducted as a form of critical conversation about what was right and good amongst all those able to participate meaningfully in this conversation. For a moment, "It became possible to recognise society in the relationships and organisations created for sustaining life and to bring these into public relevance by bringing them forward as interests for public discussion and/or the action of the state" (Calhoun 1992, p. 9). At this time, following the decline of the feudal public sphere, but before the ossification and corruption of the bourgeois public sphere, Habermas's ideal bourgeois public sphere existed.

The Refeudalisation of the Public Sphere

The reign of an enlightening bourgeois public sphere was destined not to last due to its inherent contradictions. The political task of the bourgeois public sphere was the regulation of a civil society that was critical and capable of contributing to political development. However, "The social precondition for this 'developed' bourgeois public sphere was a market that, tending to be liberalized, made affairs in the sphere of social reproduction as much as possible a matter of private people left to themselves". This had the effect of emphasising existing power differences, and "completed the privatisation of civil society" (Habermas 1989, p. 74). With further control of the market placed in the hands of the bourgeois political realm, "the positive meaning of 'private' emerged precisely in reference to the concept of free power of control over property that functioned in a capitalist fashion" (Habermas 1989, p. 74). The bourgeoisie had supposed a certain equality in private access to the public realm that in reality simply did not exist. As a result the public realm came to be dominated by bourgeois ideals and bourgeois laws, which led to the marginalisation of "common people" from both the political public sphere and civil society.

An ambiguous commitment to political participation was one of the inherent contradictions of the bourgeois public sphere. On one hand, the enlightenment attainable by participation in the political public sphere was to be coveted by all and available to everyone; on the other hand, only those who owned property, and thus had certain guarantees of education, were entitled to participate. The constitutional constructions of the bourgeoisie were based upon high-minded ideals of civil rights that had no grounding in the reality of social existence, in which exclusion from civil society due to economic status within that society went hand in hand with exclusion from the political realm (Habermas 1989, p. 85). However, in employing a highly rationalised civil rights argument in order to overturn the legitimacy of feudal powers, the bourgeoisie were forced to concede that if "all men are created equal" then they should all receive equal opportunity to participate in their own governance, regardless of their wealth or status. Of course, this did not reduce the structural inequalities brought about by the bourgeois design and control of the political public sphere; but it did mean "the enlargement of the public" to include those previously disenfranchised by high material prerequisites for public participation.

The expansion of the franchise was met with mixed reactions from the liberal political theorists of the time. Liberals such as Alexis De Tocqueville and John Stuart Mill appreciated the fact that the ideal public sphere would be all-inclusive; however, they also warned of the consequences of opening up democratic procedures.

> This was because the unreconciled interests which, with the broadening of the public, flooded the public sphere were represented in a divided public opinion and turned public opinion (in the form of the currently dominant opinion) into a coercive force, whereas it had once been supposed to dissolve any kind of coercion into the compulsion of reason. (Habermas 1989, p. 133)

Public opinion, as a compulsion toward conformity rather than a critical force, undermined the critical capacity of the public sphere and caused liberals such as Mill to deplore "the yoke of public opinion" that could stifle critical debate (Habermas 1989, p. 133). The contradictions inherent in the bourgeois public sphere thus led to a further "transformation" of the public sphere.

The expansion of the franchise can be understood to have led to a new role for public debate. Marx had held high hopes that given access to the public sphere the masses would transform it into "what, according to liberal pretence, it had always claimed to be", a universal forum for expression and discussion (Habermas 1989, p. 177). However, Habermas points out that "the occupation of the political public sphere by the unpropertied masses led to an interlocking of state and society which removed from the public sphere its former basis without supplying a new one" (Habermas 1989, p. 177). The unifying private interests of the constituents of the bourgeois public had been overwhelmed by a self-interested, non-critical and widely divergent public. The public realm became the staging point for expressions of private interest, and negotiating material interests became the role of the public forum.

The shift in the role of public debate can be seen in the rise of the Chartist movement in 19th century Britain and Ireland. The Chartists, seeking to expand the franchise beyond the bourgeoisie, sought to highlight the political exclusion of the working class so that they might have some representation in the political process. The way in which the Chartists pursued this aim was to organise petitions signed by the disenfranchised masses—many petitions gaining well over a million signatures. However, while the Chartists did eventually gain their goal in 1918, the nature of public debate had been altered substantially. In the place of rational debate between adversaries where the force of the better argument carried the day, the expansion of the franchise led to political discussion being dominated by those who represented the interests of the greatest numbers. Political participation was extended to all, but the expression of that participation was reduced to a massive, anonymous tabulation of numbers. With this, the political system became oriented by utility, rather than by reason.

This new role of the public realm as a space for the mediation of private interests resulted in the emergence of welfare state mass democracy. The dominance of competing interests resulted in the private economic affairs of citizens being the central public concern, and the most legitimate justification of statehood came in the form of state care of the private affairs of its citizens (Habermas 1989, p. 158). At the same time the financial demands of the welfare state made economic prosperity the predetermined goal of the political system. Here society and the state became intertwined. In the formal political realm, publicity, in the sense of critical scrutiny of the state, gave way to public relations, mass-mediated staged displays and the manufacture and manipulation of public opinion (Fraser 1992, p. 113). Meanwhile private organisations began to assume increasing public power as powerbrokers in the political realm (Calhoun 1992, p. 21). The public sphere became the realm of private affairs, and the private sphere—issues of household economics—assumed a disproportionate public relevance, thus completing the structural transformation of the public sphere.

The outcome of this structural transformation, for Habermas, is a "refeudalisation" of the public sphere. Habermas points out that in modern democratic society "rational-critical debate has a tendency to be replaced by consumption, and the web of public communication unravels into acts of individuated reception, however uniform in mode" (Habermas 1989, p. 161). Rather than presenting us with the opportunity to engage in critical debate, the elevation of private issues to the centre of public debate makes us regard the public realm as consumers. The public becomes a place for the representation of images and symbols. The people are engaged—only insofar as they anonymously tabulate their allegiance—but the ability to set public agendas falls once again to the elites. In this we see the "refeudalisation" of the public sphere—where all publicity is about managing representations through spectacles which keep the citizens in awe of the established systems of power.

The Role of the Media in the Refeudalised Public Sphere

The key to this notion of refeudalisation is the return to a "representative publicity" to which the public responds with conspicuous consumption within the public realm, as opposed to critical engagement with it. "The sounding board of an educated stratum tutored in the public use of reason", which once provided the basis for the rise of bourgeois democracy, "has been shattered" (Habermas 1989, p. 175). In its place exists a public that "is split apart into minorities of specialists who put their reason to use nonpublicly and the great mass of consumers whose receptiveness is public but non-critical" (Habermas 1989, p. 175). As Habermas points out, this form of publicity is a complete contradiction of the original intention of the bourgeois democrats, as it lacks communication amongst members of a public and manifests a public sphere where private interests are displayed and contested publicly.

The result of this refeudalisation is an intertwining of state and society that blurs the notions of public and private. As the public sphere became the battleground of diverse private interests the state assumed the function of social guarantor, as opposed to the forum of social debate. The role of the state has "evolved" so that it ensures that every citizen can meet the basic requirements of bourgeois (material) existence (Habermas 1989, pp. 146–148). The result of this shift to welfare state democracy means that issues of private survival replace the normative element of public debate (envisioned as the *raison d'etre* of the bourgeois public sphere by thinkers such as Kant as the central concern of the state. As a result:

> The public sphere becomes a setting for states and corporate actors to develop legitimacy not by responding appropriately to an independent and critical public but by seeking to instil in social actors motivations that conform to the needs of the overall system dominated by those states and corporate actors. (Calhoun 1992, p. 26)

This removal of the critical function of the democratic state underpins Habermas's problem with modern democracies—that being that the public realm facilitated by the mass media is oriented towards its own systemic success, rather than any responsibility to act as a public sphere.

As evidenced in *The Structural Transformation of the Public Sphere*, Habermas's main criticism of modern liberal democracies is that they allow great advantage to certain groups under the guise of equal participation. The possibility of a truly critical public sphere is frustrated by the fact that certain groups hold disproportionate power over the formation and manipulation of public opinion. This is a manifestation of one of the initial contradictions of the bourgeois public sphere; formal equality in civil society and public life does not translate to equality in the actually existing world. To put it bluntly, the average individual has less chance of influencing public opinion than the owner of a newspaper. As the public sphere becomes a forum for private issues, as opposed to public ones, media becomes a field for business advertising and, as a result, "private people as owners of property [have] a direct effect on private people as the public" (Habermas 1989, p. 189). The bourgeois democratic ethos involves gestures toward the ideal of a civil society of free and equal participation. However, the structural transformation of the public sphere exaggerates the distinction between those who have expressive access to publicity and the masses who, without expressive access, can only involve themselves publicly as consumers.

Habermas argues that the undue influence of certain groups over the public realm of the contemporary liberal public sphere was facilitated by bourgeois control of the mass media. "News" originated from the needs of business interests and the notion that the mass media should serve the interest of the wealthy was enshrined in the new public realms of bourgeois democracy.

> Ever since the marketing of the editorial section became interdependent with that of
> the advertising section, the press (until then an institution of private people insofar as
> they constituted a public) became an institution of certain participants in the public
> sphere in their capacity as private individuals; that is, it became the gate through
> which privileged private interests invaded the public sphere. (Habermas 1989, p. 185)

The dominance of business interests in the mass media rendered control of the content of the media to the bourgeois class. The result was that the material dominance of the bourgeoisie was translated into their practical dominance of the lifeworld.

The commercialised nature of the mass media has inevitably affected the quality of the kind of deliberation available to the public. Habermas cites an early study of American media which shows that even in the early penny press sales were maximised by the purposeful exclusion of political content that might alienate potential readers (and buyers) (Bleyer 1927, p. 184). The market demands "immediate reward news" such as "tales of corruption, humour, accidents, disasters and social events, rather than 'delayed reward news' of critical social issues" (Habermas 1989, pp. 169–170). The content of media designed for consumption cannot be too challenging for its audience, or it runs the risk of losing both the audience and its advertising revenue. "Radio stations, publishers and associations have turned the staging of panel discussions into a flourishing secondary business", Habermas notes. "Thus, discussion seems to be carefully cultivated and there seems to be no barrier to its proliferation. But surreptitiously it has changed in a specific way: it assumes the form of a consumer item" (Habermas 1989, p. 164). The practical result of this is that civil society comes to be dominated by forms of media that are oriented towards consumption rather than towards rational critical debate.

Habermas argues that this orientation towards consumption rather than expression signals a return to the feudal notion of publicity, in which the expressive boundaries of participation are set prior to the conversation (Habermas 1989, p. 164). As with the feudal era, the business owners who maintain the contemporary public realm do so with a view to maintaining the status quo and, to that end, they purposefully alter public interaction to be consumptive rather than critical. In the world of advertising publicity is coveted in order to generate consumption, and does so through the "reorientation of public opinion by the formation of new authorities or symbols which will have acceptance" (Steinberg 1958, p. 92). Just as with the feudal era, it is the very absence of critical public debate that gives such "authorities and symbols" their power and it is those with control over mediatised publics that benefit from being able to establish such symbols. We express our public spirit in a public world established by private corporations, where we are given the impression that we may actually make a difference in the world they have shaped for us[3]. At the same time we do not expect to affect the structure of the political public realm, where we ironically feel unqualified to debate issues of public importance; instead we may only take sides through consumption.

Habermas argues that the exaggerated public influence of the bourgeoisie manifests itself not only in the realm of civil society, but also in the political public sphere. The structural transformation of the public sphere resulted in a change in the function of parliament from being a forum for critical debate to being a forum for the negotiation of social interests. The bourgeoisie had to make certain concessions to the numerical superiority of the newly enfranchised proletariat; hence the emergence of parliament as a forum for social bargaining resulted in a more equitable distribution of state wealth. However, the bourgeoisie retained the constitutionally guarded rights and representative democratic system that ensured their continual dominance of civil society. The result of this compromise was welfare state mass democracy; "making proletarian life bearable and ensuring the gap between the rich and the poor did not grow so big that the poor could not afford the products of the rich" (Habermas 1989, p. 146). The emergence of welfare state mass democracy incorporated the proletarian class into a state whose civil society is dominated by the bourgeoisie.

This emergence of welfare state democracy resulted in a fundamental shift in the purpose of parliament's publicity. Parliamentarians were judged on their ability to represent their constituents' private interests as opposed to their ability to participate in rational-critical debate (Habermas 1989, p. 180)[4]. Citizens, therefore, regarded the parliament as stakeholders, and adopted "a general attitude of demand" (Habermas 1989, p. 211). This attitude is inherently associated with bourgeois influence upon civil society. "Because private enterprises evoke in their customers the idea that in their consumption they act in their capacity as citizens, the state has to 'address' its citizens like consumers" (Habermas 1989, p. 195). In other words, governments have to compete with private enterprise in presenting a consumable product. The ideal of providing a forum of debate is so remote that Habermas suggests the most effective political party would be one without members or platforms "but [which] mobilizes only in the event of an election in the same manner as an advertising agency with no other goal than to win that election" (Habermas 1989, pp. 200–211). The mercenary nature of this system can be seen in the fact that "'independent voters' who know and care the least, are nevertheless the target of election campaigns" (Habermas 1989, p. 215). Mass-mediated welfare state democracy thereby completes the transformation of the public sphere from a realm of critical debate to a realm of consumption.

Following this exploration of *The Structural Transformation of the Public Sphere* it is easy to see that Habermas held a dim view of the critical capacities created by the structure of contemporary democracy. Reflecting on the failure of the public sphere to uncover the errors within the September dossier on Saddam Hussein's Weapons of Mass Destruction program, it's clear that following the decline of the bourgeois public sphere neither parliament nor the media can really be understood to provide a forum for critical interrogation of political decisions. Each forum, each system, is focused on its own success—success which is measured through consumption rather than critical analysis. Habermas stresses that if there is any hope for contemporary democracy it is in further incorporating democratic forms into societal organisation; but he remains pessimistic about the possibility of this in a society in which the mode of appropriation "removed the ground for a communication about what had been appropriated" (Habermas 1989, p. 227 & 116). While it is easy to blame the system(s) for the failure in public communication, it's equally important to understand that these failures also lead to—and in many cases, propagate—citizens' declining interest in public affairs.

Arendt, Media Effects and the Alienation of Public Action

Arendt's position on why modern citizens are not interested in public life arises from the lack of opportunity they are given to express themselves. One of the most fundamental challenges to the dominance of the agonistic model of a public realm over those of *animal laborans* and *homo faber* is that the vast majority of citizens are far more familiar with the world of work or labour than they are with the world of action. Arendt's visions of the "good life" are a good example of the case in point. Based as they are on the teachings of ancient philosophers and pieced together through Arendt's own abstract thought, they are neither accessible nor interesting to the vast majority of modern citizens. Indeed, the majority of citizens "will generally judge public activities in terms of their usefulness to supposedly higher ends—to make the world more useful and beautiful in the case of *homo faber*, to make life easier and longer in the case of *animal laborans*" (Arendt 1958, p. 108). The point here is that the quality of the public we engage with determines the way in which we engage as a public. As Habermas points out, as the media has developed in its role as public medium, it has tended to regard citizens primarily as consumers, rather than an active and expressive public. We have become estranged from the notion that we ought to be expressing ourselves through our thought and speech and as a result we are somewhat alienated from Arendt's ideal version of public life.

Arendt and Models of Mass Media Effects

Perhaps the most immediate example of Arendt's alienation from public life can be found in the manner in which modern mass media technology isolates individuals and thus primes them for the reception of media messages. Looking at the dominant communication technologies of mass media—radio, television, film and newspaper—it is apparent that the technologies are designed in order to facilitate one-way, exclusive communication where reception is highly individuated. With such technologies, the opportunity to speak or act in response to the media message is incredibly limited. The result is that the consumption of modern mass media can heighten our degree of isolation. This isolation is ideal for limiting the access to public communication and extending the impact of media messages. In *The Origins of Totalitarianism* Hannah Arendt identified that:

> Isolation is that impasse into which men are driven when the political sphere of their lives, where they act together in the pursuit of a common concern, is destroyed. Yet isolation, though destructive of power and the capacity for action, not only leaves intact but is required for all so-called productive activities of men. (Arendt 1967, p. 474)

The broadcast nature of mass media technology is perfectly honed for an isolated and passive audience. Much of this is down to the technology itself—speakers, screens and newsprint are designed for a one-way flow of communication—from speaker to receiver. Gone are the opportunities for inclusion and questioning which are requirements for ideal forms of communication. Also removed is the capacity for the receiver to express themselves as part of the communication process. The result of this is that media audiences are, through the very nature of their participation, conditioned to be silent, isolated, receivers of information.

One way of understanding this relationship between the qualities of the public sphere and the qualities of the individuals is to investigate how this situation relates to models of media effects. Of the four traditional mass media effects models, two suggest that the media plays an important role in shaping social and individual behaviour—the other two emphasise the role of external influences in moderating media effects. The first model of media effects is the Magic Bullet, or Hypodermic Needle, model. This model developed from the

Frankfurt School's early estimations of media effects in a media environment dominated by government propaganda. It suggests that media have a direct and discernable influence upon the receiver, and is concerned that communication is one directional, comes from a position of power and authority (because only the powerful have the wealth necessary to produce and disseminate media messages) and is often defined by its use of persuasive communication. According to this model, the media play a central role in establishing the conditions which govern our public action. This understanding of media effects is presented in the following quote from Horkheimer and Adorno's essay on "The Culture Industry":

> The most intimate reactions of human beings have been so thoroughly reified that the idea of anything specific to themselves now persists only as an utterly abstract notion: personality scarcely signifies anything more than shining white teeth and freedom from body odour and emotions. The triumph of advertising in the culture industry is that consumers feel compelled to buy and use its products even though they see through them. (Horkheimer & Adorno 1987, p. 167)

Arendt would no doubt sympathise with Horkheimer and Adorno about the dangers of media exposure; however, understanding why media can effectively compel citizens to identify with the interests of private companies is far more involved than a simple and direct effect.

The second model outlined here is that of Selective Perception, which was developed by Berelson and Steiner (1964), amongst others, in response to the magic bullet model. Following the growth of behavioural studies into media effects following the Second World War, it became readily apparent that the effect of media was differentiated by pre-existing audience attitudes towards the particular media message being presented. It was found that if a media message ran contrary to strongly held pre-existing beliefs or values of the receiver, then through the combined processes of selective attention and selective perception, the viewer was unlikely to be affected by the message. This line of research explained why some people were affected by certain media messages, whilst others were not. It also led to generalisations about who was likely to be affected by media messages—being those who were less likely to hold pre-existing values and beliefs; or in other words, those who did not have a strong sense of their own individuality. When one considers Arendt's insistence upon the immediacy of the public sphere it becomes clear that insofar as mass media technologies transform public interaction into a mode of isolated and individuated reception, it is more likely that individuals who are exposed to a mass media-dominated public sphere are less likely to hold strong pre-existing values and beliefs, as they lack access to a public interaction which would validate their identity and values as somehow real.

The very mode of communication can be understood to affect the human capacity to form judgment about that communication.

The third model of media effects is Social Learning Theory, principally outlined by Albert Bandura and Richard Walters (1963). Social learning theory developed from the insights that informed the selective perception model and emphasised the role that external social influences have upon the effect of media messages. In this model, congruence between activities and behaviour seen on television with those experienced in real life heightens the effect of television messages. For instance, if media continually give you the impression that an expensive car is an attribute of success and then you notice that people you consider successful in the real world drive expensive cars, you are more likely to accept that an expensive car is an attribute of success. Conversely, if people you considered successful drove a rust bucket, or no car at all, you're less likely to accept that expensive cars are an attribute of success. The influence of the mass-mediated public sphere on this model of media effects is readily apparent. If you're in a situation where the majority of opinion leaders and trusted communicators take their cues from the mass media, the congruence between social and mediated experience is likely to be high, resulting in a higher level of media effects. Once again, Arendt's point is that because we rarely come together in public spaces which might challenge the perception of reality generated by the media, we lose faith in our own ability to successfully determine what is "real" and become more susceptible to accepting the influence of the media.

The final model of mass media effects—Cultivation Theory—suggests that exposure to media gradually, over time, changes social expectations about the world. Cultivation theory research has shown that prolonged exposure to consistent media messages has the power to affect our beliefs about what the world is "really" like (Gerbner, Gross, Morgan, & Signorielli 1986, pp. 19–20). Thus, prolonged exposure to violent acts on the evening news can cause frequent viewers to believe that the world is more violent and dangerous than it really is—a phenomenon called "mean world syndrome". This model resonates with Habermas's perception of the systemic colonisation of the lifeworld. Because sensational news and good looking people (for example) are better for ratings than "normalcy", we see more of both in the media. After prolonged exposure, our perception of reality is warped as a result. This model recognises the important role that our public world plays in establishing what we consider "real". If that public world is contorted by a preconceived interest in profit, utility or sensationalism, then that is bound to have an effect on individuals' perception of reality.

So we see, following this cursory examination of media effects models, that there is some consensus about the effects of media upon social behaviours. While the extent of media effects are certainly differential, based upon the audience's pre-existing values and beliefs; the more the media plays a role in shaping, and is consistent with, the audience's lifeworld, the more effective media is likely to be. The rise of the mass media as a communicative force in contemporary society signals the loss of an expressive, plural public world where we can come to understand reality in a cooperative search for the truth. Instead, with the increasing influence of the mass media in the public sphere we find public communication tends to be one directional, profit oriented and treats the individual as a passive receiver of information. This final point—the lack of opportunity for individuals to expressively engage with the construction of their "reality" (or what Habermas would call their "lifeworld")—is the reason that mass media has an unprecedented opportunity to influence the values and beliefs of individuals. Because we lack a public space which facilitates thought, speech and expressive action, we find that the privately coopted "public" media encourages nothing more than expression through the profitable pursuits of production and consumption (Arendt 1958, p. 133).

The Alienation of Public Action

Arendt suggests the modern public realm can never truly move beyond its mire because it only allows for expression through either production or consumption. In a society in which status is derived not from public life but from earning and spending power, value—both material and human—exists only insofar as the yardstick of consumption and production can measure it. Arendt argues that the possibilities for action in such a society are limited to the purchase and control of commodities and, as a result, any gains achieved from excess production can only be meaningfully invested through a corresponding increase in consumption (Arendt 1958, pp. 124–131). The permanence of material possessions provides *homo faber* with the only recourse to some form of immortality or meaning in the world. Without a public outlet for disclosing action, possession of material objects fulfils the role of public disclosure of identity.

One consequence of such an existence is a waste economy, in which people, who understand production and consumption as their only standards of meaning, regard all objects as consumable goods. The objectification of all meaning, and the status of material goods as the sole recourse of man to immortality, "harbours the great danger that eventually no object of the world will be safe from consumption or annihilation through consumption" (Arendt 1958, p. 133).

> The tragedy is that in the moment *homo faber* seems to have found fulfilment in terms of his own activity, he begins to degrade the world of things, the end product of his own mind or hands; if man the user is the highest end, 'the measure of all things', then not only nature, treated by *homo faber* as the almost 'worthless material'; upon which to work, but the 'valuable' things themselves have become mere means, thereby losing their own intrinsic 'value'. (Arendt 1958, p. 155)

Caught in the situation where we see our value in material possessions but no intrinsic value either in ourselves or in "unprocessed" material, we run the risk of replicating the tragedy of the commons, whereby we regard everything only in terms of its use value and assume the only justifiable uses for material are our own private ends—a situation which quickly results in the absolute degradation of everything that could otherwise be shared[5].

In the end, the most disturbing fact is that there is no public sphere that might stimulate critical thought and thus facilitate an escape from this situation. The logical political forum for a society numerically dominated by *homo faber* and *animal laborans* is a utilitarian democracy, insofar as it functions to efficiently provide the decisions conducive to the greatest utility; and indeed this model of democracy is not only present in modern societies, it is hegemonic in world politics. The result of the search for utility in government gives rise to an essentially uncritical public sphere. In accordance with the rise of the philosophy of *homo faber*, politics has been reduced from the role of normative contemplation to that of legitimating the state's distribution of wealth and productive capacities. *Animal laborans* seeks to fulfil needs and wants in the life process, and *homo faber* seeks to achieve validation through the production and consumption of material to satisfy these needs. What is never acknowledged in the political realm is the need for a separate space for action, or even the legitimacy of any challenge to the current status quo.

The numeric and ideological dominance of the ideals of *homo faber* and *animal laborans* gives rise to "the transformation of the public space of politics into a pseudospace of social interaction, in which individuals no longer 'act' but 'merely behave' as economic producers, consumers and urban city dwellers" (Benhabib 1990, p. 169). Most importantly for Arendt, the fact that no space is generated to encourage the development of thinking, acting and speaking has cataclysmic outcomes.

> The reason why it may be wise to distrust the political judgment of scientists *qua* scientists is not primarily their lack of 'character'—that they did not refuse to develop atomic weapons—or their naïveté—that they did not understand that once these weapons were developed they would be the last to be consulted about their use—but

precisely the fact that they move in a world where speech has lost its power. And whatever men do or know or experience can make sense only to the extent that it can be spoken about. (Arendt 1958, p. 4)

An understanding of the importance of thinking and acting in Arendt's thought helps to identify why she judges public space in terms of its conduciveness towards thought, speech and action. Her criticism of modern democratic systems is based on the understanding that, through a preconceived notion of the utilitarian purpose of public space, modern democracies marginalise free expression and reduce their potential as a place for disclosure and critical discussion. Because we have allowed issues of function and utility to dominate our public space, we are less likely to be thoughtful, critical and expressive in these spaces, and we are more likely to encourage the development of non-critical, utility maximisers in the mould of Adolf Eichmann.

Conclusion

Arriving at the end of our investigation of deliberative and agonistic understandings of the problems of modern liberal democracy, we are left with largely consistent indications as to how we might expect to overcome these deficiencies. A public culture of critical engagement is central to Arendt's and Habermas's solutions to the critical deficit of democratic systems, and each suggests that the cultivation of "ideal" forums is integral to addressing the broad social problems brought about by the ascendancy of instrumentalism and the decline of critical thought. Both agonistic and deliberative theorists identify a similar malaise in liberal democracies—being an inadequate critical impetus in the functioning of democratic institutions. However, they have somewhat different ideas about how this inadequacy ought to be rectified. Habermas tries to incorporate critical deliberation into the very procedure of communication. Arendt, on the other hand, seeks to inspire critical thought by creating a space for the celebration of the human faculties of thought, speech and action. Habermas's approach is to try and make an irrefutable and always evocable connection between public power and the critique of that power. Arendt's approach is to seek to institute publics that inspire thought and criticism through participation[6]. One thing I hope I have shown is that these differences do not render agonistic and deliberative theories incompatible. Indeed, given their shared understanding of the communicative composition of power, it is easy to understand that critical engagement with the "space" for communication and the "mode" of communication comes to constitute the same thing—an individual's expressive interaction with discursively constituted power. It is not that democracies need to become more critical *or* engaging; democracies need to be more critical *and* engaging in order to fulfil the aspirations of agonistic and deliberative theorists.

There are, however, also many elements of Habermas's and Arendt's work which conspire to portray a highly pessimistic view of the future of the public sphere and the related future of humanity. Chief amongst these is the effect of mass media upon our society and upon us as individuals. While an optimistic synthesis of agonistic and deliberative theories might suggest that expressive individuals will seek to constitute ideal communication in all their public interactions, there are a number of reasons to expect that advanced economies will not naturally develop into sophisticated critical democratic systems. A central concern is one which both Habermas and Arendt identify: as a result of the impoverishment of the public sphere, advanced capitalist societies have developed such a capacity to control public communication that the very human impetus for freedom and sovereignty has been undermined. Simply put, the problem is that if the public sphere plays a fundamental role in creating individuals—or in setting the boundaries of communicative power— then the more corrupted the public sphere, the more corrupted the individuals and communicative power produced by that public sphere.

PART TWO

DIGITAL SPACES: DIGITAL SELVES

Introducing the Age of the Spectacle

> This is our decision, to live fast and die young.
> We've got the vision, now let's have some fun.
> Yeah, it's overwhelming, but what else can we do?
> Get jobs in offices, and wake up for the morning commute.
>
> Forget about our mothers and our friends
> We're fated to pretend
>
> —MGMT 'Time to Pretend' (2007)

On 19 February 2003, a live broadcast from the US Secretary of Homeland Security was interrupted in order to report on efforts to save a dog stuck on an ice floe in a New Jersey river (WWB 2003). At least three US News Networks (Fox, CNN and MSNBC) judged that coverage of the stranded Rottweiler was of greater public interest than the launch of a new Homeland Security initiative and dumped the press conference for live coverage of the rescue attempt. Fox even sent a helicopter to capture the action. Such media coverage represents a new stage in the transformation of the public sphere. Public space is no longer ruled by judgments of utility or instrumentalism, the hallmarks of the modern era; now public communication is dominated by spectacles—where the sensational rules.

The age of the spectacle has arisen following the age of instrumentality which pervaded the modern era. Whereas the age of instrumentalism was dominated by the needs and interests of *homo faber*, or beings defined by making, the age of the spectacle is dominated by *homo spectaculum*—or beings defined by spectacles. The term *homo spectaculum* is one I use here to refer to the rise of a new kind of individual which has emerged following the loss of critical public space and the increase in the social influence of media voices. Following a brief introduction as to how we can account for the emergence of this new subjectivity, I shall highlight how the change in subjectivity can be witnessed as a move from instrumental rationality to "the society of the spectacle". I shall then go on to indicate how *homo spectaculum* can be understood as a product of fragmented consciousness and as a result of the replacement of public space by "private publics". Finally, I shall outline the subjectivity of *homo spectaculum* by identifying its activities, its instruments and its proclivities. By establishing a theoretical image of *homo spectaculum* it is then possible to identify how *homo spectaculum* is engaged in public communication and how this subjectivity interacts with contemporary liberal democratic systems of government. Habermas and Arendt see the rise of the social and the refeudalisation of the public sphere as the end point of their analysis. In this chapter these moments will be viewed as the beginning of an examination of the ways in which the privatisation of "public" space affects the emancipatory potentials of contemporary democracy.

The development of the concept of *homo spectaculum* is influenced by Guy Debord's description of contemporary society as *The Society of the Spectacle* (Debord 1995)[1]. Whilst Arendt's description of the public realm of *homo faber* resembles what Herbert Marcuse has described as "One Dimensional Society" (Marcuse 1964), the argument I shall develop here is that this understanding of a public realm dominated by instrumentality is no longer adequate for an understanding of contemporary society. As the story of the dog rescue suggests, we are no longer interested in making the public sphere as materially, economically and politically rational as possible, instead we are happy to use the public sphere as a personal distraction, where emotion, sensation and novelty are often more important than rationalisation. Debord, along with others such as Frederick Jameson, has explained this development from instrumental publics to "publics" of display as a shift necessary for the continued expansion of capital. One way to understand this development is in terms of the increasing role and influence "privatised" public spaces play in establishing our systems of meaning. Simply put, the infiltration of spectacles into the lifeworld becomes so thorough and unproblematic that spectacles have taken the place of reality; in the popular imagination, sensation is preferable to truth.

This change in the nature of public spaces affects the possibility of the public sphere inspiring the kind of individual "heroic" citizenship which Arendt saw as the result of an ideal public sphere. When Arendt's human subjects are born into the age of the spectacle and start to create meaning, the colonised lifeworld forms the basis of individuals' shared and unproblematic convictions, and systemic forces thus come to constitute the boundaries for individuals' agonistic engagement. This engagement, however, is not purely thoughtful or communicative, as its "original position" of thought is already strategically defined by the "public" in which it is constituted. Furthermore, unlike the public realm of *homo faber*, this public realm caters to display and expression—albeit display and expression within the contexts defined by those who control "public" space. This new condition, in which the public realm engages within a predefined context, displaces Arendt's emancipatory force of action and replaces it with behaviour. This brings about a subjectivity that is not *animal laborans* (defined by its exclusion from public appearance), nor *homo faber* (defined through its fabrication within a public realm dominated by instrumental value), nor properly human (defined through expressive public action), but that of *homo spectaculum*—humans defined through their performance in a manufactured spectacle.

Fragmented Publics, Fragmented Individuals

In Arendtian terms, the loss of a shared public undermines the impetus for individuals to express themselves consistently. The very term "individual" refers to the non-divisible nature of the ideal modern citizen—a citizen who behaves consistently according to their beliefs and thoughts about what constitutes a good life. As has been well documented by writers such as Michel Foucault, the modern period distinguished itself by its efforts to discipline individuals through the use of space and surveillance (Foucault 1975). The modern institutions of schools and prisons were very much an attempt to imbue citizens with the discipline necessary to behave well on a consistent basis—to become individual was to become consistent. This is the same process which Kant referred to as being the basis for the Enlightenment (and for what he hoped would be a "perpetual peace") whereby citizens encouraged to think well, would go on to live well in all aspects of their lives. What follows is an explanation of how the loss, or fragmentation, of public spaces in liberal democracies has led to a concurrent decline in individuality. From fragmented publics has arisen a new fragmented individual—no longer consistent but "dividual" and adaptable.

The Loss of a Plural Public: *Homo Faber's* Abstraction from Reality

As described in the first chapter, Arendt believes that *homo faber's* obsession with instrumentality contributes to an impoverished public existence. In a public realm dominated by the values of *homo faber* we find a society obsessed with rationalisation, where utility is the equivalent of meaningfulness and human purpose is equated to production. Herbert Marcuse identifies this type of instrumentalist repression in his work *One Dimensional Man* (Marcuse 1964). The chief characteristic of one dimensional subjectivity is

> the repression of all values, aspirations, and ideas which cannot be defined in terms
> of the operations and attitudes validated by the prevailing forms of rationality. The
> consequence is the weakening and even the disappearance of all genuinely radical
> critique, the integration of all opposition in the established condition.[2]

Like Arendt, Marcuse criticises the thoughtlessness of a public realm dominated by instrumental rationality. Marcuse also makes the Arendtian argument that in coming to dominate the public realm, instrumental rationality has concurrently come to generate its own reality. What was public, or rather what could be publicly acknowledged, was regarded through a single instrumental rationality. This signifies the "absorption of ideology into reality" such that the ideology of instrumentality comes to define reality (Marcuse 1964, p. 11). Under the public dominance of *homo faber* instrumentality comes to represent that public's "communistic fiction" or "invisible hand" that provides universal values and aspiration for citizens and in doing so marginalises all other forms of engagement (Arendt 1958, pp. 44-45).

In contrast, Arendt's human and worldly publics are open to plurality and inherently multidimensional because

> the conditions of human existence—life itself, natality and morality, worldliness,
> plurality, and the earth—can never 'explain' what we are or answer the question of
> who we are for the simple reason that they never condition us absolutely. (Arendt
> 1958, p. 11)

Marcuse indicates, however, that following the acceptance of instrumental reason as the sole basis for public legitimacy, there is no opportunity for those "differently conditioned" to engage in debate. Whereas reality had previously been defined by "what everyone can publicly agree upon", reality was now constructed by a system of rationality which, as a dominant ideology, determined the conditions of public agreement. Arendt recognises that the consciousness of *homo faber* was the first to generate reality from the Archimedean point, beyond the earth and beyond the plurality of human existence (Arendt 1958, p. 11). Marcuse aptly describes the myopia produced by this situation in its nascent state—instrumentalism and engagement through material reality was the ideology that, as a result of its own inherent means-ends tendencies, came to recreate society based upon an abstraction. One dimensional society, therefore, signals the emergence of ideology as reality.

Whereas Marcuse and Arendt are concerned with the public dominance of a particular form of reason, Habermas's theoretical progression displays an increasing preoccupation with the loss of public ideology altogether. Marcuse is in agreement with Arendt on this particular point: instrumentality was the first step in rationalisation that detached public meaning from its determination in public. According to Arendt, this was a fundamental shift, as prior to the rise of instrumentality, reality had been determined as a result of plural, real, consistent identities agreeing on something. According to Marcuse the rise of instrumentality represented the dominance of single (instrumental) rationality over the public sphere. Habermas, however, describes this conception as obsolete. He suggests that rather than a single public sphere and a single ideology that eventually would conflict with the limited productive imperatives of the lifeworld, contemporary society has developed a "functional equivalent to ideology formation" that avoids the productive constraints generated by having to be consistent (Habermas 1987b, p. 355). The use of the term "functional" implies the instrumental origins that underpin the development of *homo spectaculum*; the use of the term "equivalent", however, clearly implies that this is no longer ideology itself. In this formulation society has undermined its own rational *and* ideological foundations in order to remain productive.

Habermas and the Fragmentation of Consciousness

Habermas, subsequently, provides us with a reasonable explanation for why private spaces have proliferated as meaning givers, while larger ideological "publics" seem to be in decline. Habermas believes that such a change began with the linguistification of the sacred, which in turn led to a compelling incredulity towards all traditional forms of legitimation. Whilst he is very rarely credited with having postmodern insights, his criticism of the subsequent fate of consciousness is an excellent introduction to the rise of the new subjectivity of *homo spectaculum*.

In a chapter of *Communicative Action* entitled "Linguistification of the Sacred", Habermas describes a process of rationalisation whereby the effort to rationally understand myths leads to their deconstruction and incredulity with respect to their legitimacy. What he refers to as "linguistification" is an abandonment of traditional structures of legitimation for rationalised structures of legitimation. As seen in the second chapter, these new forms of legitimacy came to undermine and usurp the coherence of preceding forms of legitimacy and led to the differentiation between system and lifeworld. One outcome of this development is that individuals themselves become fragmented.

> To the degree that the Protestant ethic of the calling ceased to place its stamp on the private conduct of life, the methodical-rational way in which the bourgeois strata led their lives was displaced by the utilitarian life-style of 'specialists without spirit' and the aesthetic-hedonistic life-style of 'sensualists without heart', that is, by two

> complementary ways of life that soon became mass phenomena. The two life-styles can be strikingly represented by different personality types, but they can also take hold of the same person. *With this fragmentation of the person, individuals lose their ability to give their life histories a certain degree of consistent direction.* (Habermas 1987b, p. 323) [my italics]

The loss of meaning is profound in that it undermines the value of a consistent identity. Without a coherent and meaningful public ideology around which to orient themselves, individuals seek meaning through various fragmented arenas of engagement. This change in the nature of public engagement represents a shift from instrumentality to spectacle. Instrumentality retains an orientation towards overall productivity by making productivity the source of all meaning. The spectacle maximises productivity by initially removing all universal orientations toward meaning[3], and then caters to the unrequited need for meaning in a way that indulges the human proclivity to display within a series of privately controlled "public" spaces.

According to Habermas, therefore, the loss of a consistent public space does not undermine the need for the meaning and context providing faculties of public space. However, he argues that the drive for meaning providing contexts is distorted and channelled into fragments in order to avoid the conflict between lifeworld and system that a consistent identity or ideology might demand.

> If...the rationalized lifeworld more and more loses its structural possibilities for ideology formation, if the facts that speak for an instrumentalizing of the lifeworld can hardly be interpreted away any longer and ousted from the horizon of the lifeworld, one would expect that the competition between forms of social and system integration would openly come to the fore. But the late capitalist societies fitting the description of 'welfare-state pacification' do not confirm this conjecture. They have evidently found some functional equivalent for ideology formation. In place of the positive task of meeting a certain need for interpretation by ideological means, we have the negative requirement of preventing holistic interpretations from coming into existence...*Everyday consciousness* is robbed of its power to synthesise, it becomes *fragmented*. (Habermas 1987b, pp. 354–355)

Here Habermas presents the profound idea that the reason that late capitalist systems are able to avoid cataclysmic change is because of a change in the conditions of individual subjectivity. "In place of 'false consciousness' we today have 'fragmented consciousness' that blocks enlightenment by the mechanism of reification" (Habermas 1987b, p. 355). Put simply, we are no longer taught to expect coherent public reason but to expect subjective private material satisfaction. As a result *homo spectaculum* refrains from questioning the legitimacy or reality of the world and instead approaches the world as a source of sensation and private gratification.

The Plight of Agonism

Understanding agonism is integral to understanding the rise of *homo spectaculum*. Agonism is crucial in providing people with an interest in maintaining a healthy and vibrant public sphere, as it is only in light of plurality that identity and public interest can be understood to be real. What has changed following the colonisation of the lifeworld is a fundamental perversion of reality, a result of the world-alienation of contemporary life. For *homo spectaculum* displays a startling lack of concern for reality. Following the public ascension of "knowing", critical public spaces are shut down. Following the elimination of critical public space, reality, in an Arendtian sense, is driven to extinction. With the loss of a forum that can be claimed to allow for a critical and plural reality the positive element of agonism is lost. If there is no public space that is truly plural, then people will be reluctant to reveal themselves in a purely expressive way. Under these conditions, display becomes a form of behaviour, as opposed to an opportunity for expression. The distinction between agonism invested in action and agonism invested in behaviour is fundamental to understanding the passive elements of *homo spectaculum's* display, so with the help of the work of John Stuart Mill, Frederick Nietzsche and Michel Foucault I shall now investigate this difference.

The need to distinguish between display as expression and display as behaviour reflects the need to understand the emancipatory potential of agonism. The agonistic drive serves as a fundamental component of the faith Arendt has in natality the irrepressible act of creating something new. She believes that in the process of founding, humans will tend to invest themselves in public and they will tend to do so critically, actively seeking to declare and defend one's privately formed ideals in a communicative way. For Arendt, the benefit of a coherent and constant identity is that it is consistently seen as the same in public and, as a result, this identity is in the most profound sense real. An expressive display of self is, therefore, a contribution to the plurality of public space. Such an identity must be generated through private reflection but seeks an ideal public in order to engage with the world in a way that validates the self in the most real (critical) and amicable (engaged) way possible. However, a passive display of self (one that evidences behaviour as opposed to expression) does nothing more than reinforce the non-plural and non-critical elements of public appearance.

The persistence of a coherent and constant identity is fundamental to Arendt's political thought, hence her motivation to describe the ideal polis as a way to express and celebrate this identity. She urges people to be proud of "that untaught and natural feeling of identity with whatever we happen to be by accident of birth" (Arendt 1959, p. 179). This cherishing of identity is a result of her high regard for natality as a critical force and her assumption that we are all the same yet different, "that is, human, in such a way that nobody is ever the same as anyone else who ever lived, lives or will live" (Arendt 1958, p. 8). She believed, following Heidegger, that being has an urge to disclose itself; hence a "good" life is one that can be told as a consistent, inspirational narrative (Arendt 1973, p. 105). Such a life would bring forth the uniqueness of one's identity most emphatically in public space, and subsequently the ideal polis, with its critical and aesthetic functions, would gratify this urge in the most socially advantageous way.

Arendt's faith in a human urge to disclose their unique selves probably stems from her personal conviction that "a philosophy of life that does not arrive, as did Nietzsche, at the affirmation of 'eternal recurrence' as the highest principle of all being, simply does not know what it is talking about" (Arendt 1958, p. 97)[4]. Arendt passionately affirms public individuality as that means by which we avoid the pitfalls of knowing and maintain the emancipatory moments of natality, critical engagement and founding. In the world of *homo spectaculum*, however, public space has been completely occluded by private space. This means that, when we examine the role of public space, we find that *expressive* forms of display are defined as useless, shunned and excluded. Instead we find the proliferation of display as behaviour, as an indication of allegiance and a way of establishing the reality of what is already known.

This kind of display as behaviour has been more thoroughly explored in the political theories of John Stuart Mill and Frederick Nietzsche. Each of these theorists identifies a human tendency to accept and rely upon a non-critical reception of the reality of the world as it is. In the tendency towards a passive reception of reality and the human predilection towards *ressentiment*, Mill and Nietzsche enable insight into the way in which *homo spectaculum* seeks to find meaning following the loss of Arendt's idealised critical public sphere.

Like Arendt, John Stuart Mill argues that critical thought must in some sense be inspired by public life. In his principal work, *On Liberty*, he makes an eloquent argument for the necessity for individuals' critical involvement in public decision making, arguing that such an involvement is beneficial for both the individual and the society in which the individual moves (Mill 1991). He argues that this critical involvement must be nurtured and encouraged through the public use of reason because without such a public individuals are naturally inclined to reject their own critical voices in favour of those of other people, and because there is a fatal tendency on the parts of members of a society to stop thinking about things as soon as they become commonly accepted (Mill 1991, p. 49). As pointed out by Dana Villa, Mill made the point that

> we don't merely accept this condition, we will it with our hearts and souls. Our acceptance of what is 'unquestionable' for our class, culture, or age, provides us with the orientation and support we yearn for in an otherwise contingent and disturbingly pluralistic world. (Villa 2001, p. 80)

We seek to orient our lives around something, and the more pervasive this reality is the more comfortable we are with our identity and security. We are "encumbered selves" in the sense that we cannot imagine ourselves as ourselves without some "unquestionable orientations"[5]. In *On Liberty* Mill develops an elegant argument against the social tendency to know, outlining why such unquestionable orientations are dangerous for both society and the individual. Whilst Mill's understanding of the social benefits of individuality varies from that of Arendt[6], he expresses very similar ideas to Arendt insofar as he advocates a public space that encourages individuals to have critical access to their world as an essential part of the good life. Without such a space, he argues, there is a prolific tendency to know, rather than to think.

Frederick Nietzsche also argues that the likelihood is greatest that people will embrace common values rather than critically engage with those values. "Madness", he famously declared, "is rare in individuals—but in groups, parties, nations, and ages it is the rule" (Nietzsche 1986, aphorism 156). As Villa points out, Nietzsche contends that the collective need for obedience to authority has stunted our appreciation of our own moral and critical capacities (Villa 2001, p. 134). Furthermore, Nietzsche argues that the "death of god", which should have resulted in an increase in critical engagement, has led instead to the appropriation of weaker idols (Goodchild 1996, p. 22). The need for "orientation" is so pressing that it cannot be abandoned, it is forever assumed. In the place of an expressive and critical formulation of reality, Nietzsche identifies a process of *ressentiment*:

> a *ressentiment* experienced by creatures who, deprived as they are of the proper outlet of action are forced to find their compensation in an imaginary vengeance. While every noble morality springs from a triumphant affirmation of its own demands, the slave morality says 'no' from the very outset to what is 'outside itself', 'different from itself' and 'not itself'; and this 'no' is its creative deed. The *volte face* of the valuing standpoint—this *inevitable* gravitation to the objective instead of back to the subjective—is typical of *ressentiment*. (Nietzsche 1956, p. 170)

In place of the critical and creative possibilities of individuality, Nietzsche perceives a devotion to a herd mentality brought about by the need for a common and, in his view, base world in which people can display[7]. Such a slave mentality can be seen in humanity's "flight" from its own senses and will to the comforting reality of material and knowledge. It can also be seen in the predilection that people have towards fear as opposed to self-affirmation. Simply, Nietzsche argues that there is an inherent human weakness that leads one to locate self within an externally created context rather than to affirm a unique identity.

Hence we can see that while Mill and Nietzsche identify the need for recognition and display, both argue that for most people this engagement tends to be display as behaviour according to externally defined parameters and not as a critical and expressive display of self. As discussed in the first chapter, Arendt describes a propensity to know, rather than think, particularly where there is no public space that encourages thought. Arendt's belief that agonism is an emancipatory force reflects her faith that humans are reality seeking individuals that tend towards a critical engagement with reality as opposed to the passive reception of reality which is expressed in display as behaviour.

Crucially, the absence of a critical public does not undermine an individual's desire to excel within the context of a commonly shared world (Arendt 1990, p. 119). Indeed, as Nietzsche argued, the failure to have a real forum to act induces a mental predisposition to will such a forum and imagine one where it does not truly exist. People "deprived of the direct outlet of action, compensate by an imaginary vengeance" (Nietzsche 1956, p. 170). As one finds oneself more isolated in the world there is a tendency to grasp onto one's illusions with greater ferocity, illusions which are subsequently less likely to be shattered by public scrutiny.

The desire to display is, therefore, both the chief virtue and vice of humanity (Arendt 1990, p. 119). As a virtue it engages with reality and inserts the plurality of a private self into that reality in a way that generates thought, action and distinction. As a vice it constitutes a form of behaviour that conforms to passively accepted contexts of meaning established prior to action. Michel Foucault is one theorist who, like Arendt, identifies the endless subjective plurality of the world as an opportunity for an expression of self. "From the ideal that the self is not given to us, I think there is only one practical consequence: we have to create ourselves as works of art" (Foucault 1983, p. 237). Certainly, *homo spectaculum* seek to develop their identities in such ways as to appear functional, desirable and spectacular; but insofar as they do so within the parameters defined by a privatised public space, the art they create is derivative rather than originating in the actor.

The Emergence of the Spectacle

Critical theorist Guy Debord is one writer who sensed this change in the role and function of public space. Writing just three years after the publication of *One Dimensional Man*, Debord argues that while instrumental reason may have been the bane of modern existence, contemporary problems stem from the subsequent usurpation of reason as a totality, and the rise of the society of the spectacle (Debord 1995). According to this analysis it seems as though, in line with postmodern irony, instrumental rationality itself has outlived its usefulness. Following on from the insights of Debord, Antonio Negri and Micheal Hardt suggest that the capitalist system relies upon the continual reinvention and abstraction of "reality"; the spectacle becomes a necessary preoccupation of capitalism. The system operates not by attempting to make everyone the same but by celebrating diversity. It "recognizes existing or potential differences, celebrates them, and manages them within a general economy of command" (Hardt & Negri 2000, p. 210). In Habermasian terms, those in control of steering media are able to strategically stimulate production and consumption beyond the natural and instrumental imperatives of the lifeworld through this control. Debord argues that those in control of the steering media are tampering with reality through their ownership and control of public space. They are encompassing individuals in a space that gives them a sense of meaning and purpose in order to keep them productive and consumptive despite the lack of a real or meaningful reason for doing so.

In *The Society of the Spectacle* Debord suggests that we are living in a reality in which ideology formation and reformation is integral to the continued survival of the capitalist system[8]. As opposed to the cause of repression identified in *One Dimensional Man*, no "rationality" is allowed to dominate the public realm, as rationality, even instrumental rationality, has lost its use value.

> The spectacle corresponds to the historical moment at which the commodity completes its colonisation of social life. It is not just that the relationship to commodities is now plain to see—commodities are now all that there is to see; the world we see is the world of the commodity. (Debord 1995, p. 29)

Debord contends that the project of advanced capitalism is to "restructure society without community" (Debord 1995, p. 137) so that a society of fragmented consciousnesses can be manipulated infinitely without challenge from the lifeworld. Where Debord deviates from Marcuse is to suggest that following this rationalisation, it becomes necessary for capital to invent new ways of developing a consumptive consciousness. From an Arendtian/Habermasian perspective, the degree to which our agonism is entertained without really being engaged reflects the degree of systemic corruption of the lifeworld or the occlusion of the political by the social. In Marxist terms this is the condition of "subsumption" through which social relations are derived primarily from the machinations of capital rather than encounters with reason or reality (Negri 1989).

In Arendtian terms, following the decline of public reality, a "public void" exists and the human desire for meaning creating contexts remains to be filled. In this situation, as Habermas and Arendt suggest through their analysis of the communicative composition of power, real political power is wielded by those who colonise the lifeworld. When *homo spectaculum* comes to asking the question "why?" the market is the only form of public space through which they can seek to provide an answer. In such a world Coke stands for freedom. Virgin stands for "power for the people". Ideas have become commodified and the strategic goal of the market is limited to its own expansion.

Hence we can see that with the emergence of *homo spectaculum*, the market proliferates as a meaning provider because it has most adequately and enthusiastically catered to the agonism of consumers by distancing them from reality and providing them with a spectacle in its place. By responding to the fragmented human imperatives of desire-satisfaction and emotional fulfillment the private public realms of the market have become far more engaging for *homo spectaculum*. However, while being engaged by the spectacle of consumption, *homo spectaculum* doesn't encounter what Arendt would describe as "reality", or what Habermas would consider a lifeworld of legitimate integrity.

Defining the Age of the Spectacle

Having outlined the conditions that have led to the emergence of the subjectivity of *homo spectaculum*, I shall now define *homo spectaculum* in terms of their activity, their instruments and their relationship to the means of production. This is the first step in identifying the subjectivity of *homo spectaculum* in the world and, consequently, in understanding the effect this subjectivity has on contemporary citizenship.

The Activity of *Homo Spectaculum*: Display as Behaviour

Animal laborans labours, *homo faber* works, humans act and *homo spectaculum* displays. The activity of display, being transient, subjective and requiring an audience to be meaningful appears to have more in common with Arendt's idealisation of action than either work or labour. There is an important distinction to be made, however, between display as expression and display as behaviour. The former, lauded by Arendt, involves an investment of self that is unique and is an earnest attempt to identify that uniqueness in the world. The latter involves an aspiration to be measured according to the standards of behaviour prescribed by someone else. As in the distinction between thinking and knowing, the former involves personal introspection, negotiation and reflection; the latter involves conforming to a pattern that is established prior to the action situation.

Homo spectaculum can be defined, therefore, as a subjectivity that seeks to display identity but not in a way that is open to the plurality of a truly public realm—as we shall see the "public" realms of the age of the spectacle actually tend to be private spaces masquerading as a public. Thus *homo spectaculum* shares with *homo faber* an engagement with a facile reality and shares with *animal laborans* the inability to contribute to publicity (or reality) in any meaningful way. In order to explain this, I shall initially describe the futility of *homo spectaculum's* agonistic engagement in these terms before going on to illustrate some of the defining features of the private public existence of *homo spectaculum*.

Animal laborans, whose activity is invested in labour, always engage their agonism in forums designed to appease agonism without actually contributing to public space in an enduring way. As mentioned in the first chapter, Arendt argues that the activity of labour leaves no public manifestation. *Animal laborans'* agonism while at work is expressed through transitory contributions to their immediate environment—such as the traditions of labourers who have sung while working. Outside of employment *animal laborans'* urge to display has traditionally been engaged through expressive activities such as playing in brass bands and sporting clubs. In these activities *animal laborans* encounters visceral realms of appearance constructed purposefully in order to make engagement immediate and self-validating. Those whose daily activity is labour seek outlets everywhere through which to express themselves through action, not because their labour reflects their personal contribution to the public realm but because their labour does not do so. *Homo spectaculum* shares with *animal laborans* the experience of being personally engaged, despite the fact that this engagement has no truly public manifestation.

Unlike *animal laborans*, the work of *homo faber* manifests a public product, and therefore *homo faber* is far more likely to engage in work in an agonistic way. It is because of the tangible material qualities of the output of work, and its association with its creator, that work is so gratifying. The agonistic urges of workers, therefore, are much easier to engage in pursuit of preconceived ends. Indeed clever employers learn how to extract and use this agonism in order to increase production by encouraging competition amongst workers and highlighting workers' "ownership" of their production. Those who excel at fabrication usually do so because they invest all their desire to display in the carefully constructed "public" of their workplace, rather than in anything approaching a real public. This engagement with agonism in the workplace is a reality constituting activity; in Habermasian language, the systemic rationality becomes the rationality of the lifeworld, and the result is *homo faber*, who is devoted to the pursuit of an end without ever thinking publicly about that end. The investment of agonism in essentially privately designed spaces is also emblematic of *homo spectaculum.*

Thus we find that while agonism is a constant, each avenue of agonistic expression is usurped and appropriated by the private "public" institutions of *homo spectaculum.* It is the loss of a public realm as a forum for critical, expressive action that has led to the creation of other "publics" (be they private, corporate or social) that do cater to the agonistic drives of the individuals who constitute them. As Mill's and Nietzsche's theories suggest, agonism need not be critical. In fact there seems to be a tendency for world reception to be passive. Arendt argues that this is why we need worthy public spaces to inspire critical agonism. Critical agonism leads to ruptures and innovations that further human interests, non-critical agonism keeps human beings passive and isolated and yet productive.

The Instruments of *Homo Spectaculum*

If the telescope is the object that redefined reality in terms of instrumentality, the screen is the object that redefines reality in terms of the spectacle. Both the telescope and screen offer the opportunity to engage reality according to a perspective external to the innate human senses and each seeks to present this perspective as real. Similarly, the flatness of the screen reflects the limited dimensionality of the perspective provided by the telescope. Both serve the role of meaning givers, despite the fact that both the telescope and the screen actually serve to occlude the reality that otherwise would be determined through critical and plural communication.

Where the telescope and the screen differ is in the effect that they have on public space. For Arendt, the telescope offers a universal perspective that can be established as public reality. Its "objectivity" becomes pervasive, and the instrument becomes the sole arbiter of reality in public conversations. The screen, on the other hand, displays a projection of reality with a view to occluding public space altogether. The screen itself is two-dimensional, limited to displaying what is projected upon it. What appears on that screen is for the producer to make and, nominally, up to the viewer to choose. Through their choices as to what is displayed on the screen, reality can be tailored to suit the needs of individuals. The screen itself is not gratifying, but generally what is presented on it is placating, sympathetic and panders to an enlarged sense of the viewer's importance. The individual, therefore, comes to feel as though it is through their personal choice that they are a participant in the construction of reality, thus satiating their need for display without the associated "difficulties" of truly public revelation or personal expression.

The telescope presents the instrument as the purveyor of reality. The instrument's objectivity is what gives it its status of public truth. The screen presents the spectacle as the purveyor of reality. The role of the screen is not to present a singular pervasive truth but to prevent the observer from looking into the space behind the screen and finding a more compelling natural and plural reality there. Screens, televisions, computers, billboards, borders: all serve to inhibit our ability to see the world as it really is and advance our ability to see the world as the screen controller/director/producer wants us to. This is emblematic of *homo spectaculum* who, deprived of any contact with reality as such, is ever more eager to engage and display within a mediatised reality that is particularly responsive to their choices.

The Productive Activity of *Homo Spectaculum*

The emergence of *homo spectaculum* has seen a shift in the focus of production from creating products to creating meaning. The outcomes of Naomi Klein's research in *No Logo* (Klein 2000) were predicted by Gilles Deleuze's theoretical insight in his meditation "On Societies of Control" (Deleuze 1992). Deleuze had suggested that the capitalist system was no longer involved in production, but had moved on to marketing the product—"the factory has given way to the corporation" and "marketing has become the centre or the 'soul' of the corporation". Meanwhile, "We are taught that corporations have a soul, which is the most terrifying news in the world" (Deleuze 1992, p. 6). Those in control of capital understand that meaning can be associated with products and consumption in order to stimulate the growth of production. By continually shifting identity markers and playing with reality, capital can continue to appropriate the productive drive of agonism. This is the world of consumerism, which can be seen as a direct outgrowth of the material orientation of the public realm dominated by *homo faber* (Giddens 1994, p. 169). In one sense the meaning provided by corporations fulfils the lack of public meaning generated through the public realm of *homo faber*; in another sense the common use of marketing to create meaning occludes the possibility that meaning will be found in a real and plural public.

The notion that capitalism operates by continually redrawing the boundaries of social existence has been around since Marx suggested that "a precondition of production based on capital is…the production of a constantly widening sphere of circulation, whether the sphere itself is directly expanded or whether more points within it are created as points of production" (Marx 1973a, p. 407). Following the expansion of capitalist production to the world market, the only scope for further expansion is in the reconfiguration of existing flows of production and the conjuring of new ones. This reconfiguration of engagement necessitates the *reconfiguration* of forms of control; thus we find that the disciplinary control of *homo faber*, is superseded by the spatial control of *homo spectaculum*, characterised by the attempt to exploit and reconfigure meaning providing spaces in order to foster continual re-production and growth.

The new role of production is reflected in the new tools of production. Digital technologies are for the corporation what machinery is for the factory: the basic technological instrument of production. Yet the fact that digital technologies do not manufacture in the same manner as industrial machinery speaks volumes for the difference between the productive activity of *homo faber* and *homo spectaculum*. As Jameson pointed out, machines of the digital ensemble are tools of reproduction rather than production (Jameson 1991, p. 37). As seen in the rise of branding and the development of a hyperreal economy, machines of the new economy are engaged in "the action of knowledge upon knowledge itself as the main source of productivity" (Castells 1996, pp. 16–17). The activity of production has lost much of its value and, as Deleuze proclaimed, has been farmed out to where labour is cheapest to be coordinated at a distance (Deleuze 1992)[9]. The crucial role that digital technologies play is the role of reproduction; that of processing information, mining the lifeworld for meaning to harness the exploitable flows of desire. This is not to say that land and capital do not play a role in the distribution of wealth and power, just that the creation of the spectacle is increasingly based upon the production and control of information—not the production of material[10].

What has changed is not simply the product but the means of production and, importantly, the relationship of the worker to the means of production. The machines of the digital ensemble are far more responsive to the isolated world of the contemporary worker than the factory and machines of production ever were to the workers of the classic industrial era. The mainstay of the digital economy is the personal computer, whose screen not only tends to isolate the individual from any sort of productive chain but also indulges the expressive capacities of the user by allowing for the personalisation of the work environment. The machines themselves are adjustable to personal tastes; from hardware that enables certain processes, to desktop settings that alter the aesthetic appearance of the "workstation".

But desktop computers represent only the thin end of the wedge as far as digital technology is concerned. Laptops, personal digital assistants and mobile phones represent a new set of tools of production that in combination ensure that the personal life of the individual remains functional regardless of what space they inhabit. Advances in information and communication technologies allow the user to always have access to a screen, in every sense of the word. Moreover, the latest web technologies have ensured that what appears on these screens is more responsive and more sensitive to the interests and needs of the user. The producers and distributors of these technologies claim that they challenge the notion that labour has to be alienating, changing the relationship of the worker to the means of production from antagonism to integration. This change reflects the shift from *homo faber*, a subjectivity confined by its instrumental sense of meaning, to *homo spectaculum*, a subjectivity confined through a choice of illusions, all of which occlude the real.

A Comment on Celebrity

The role of celebrity in the society of *homo spectaculum* provides a perfect example with which to illustrate the ways in which the private publics of *homo spectaculum* differ from those of *homo faber* and Arendt's idealised Greek public. Individuals whose work involves a major contribution to spectacular space get to express their agonism in a very spectacular way. That is to say the position of public celebrity becomes fetishised in the world of *homo spectaculum*. Celebrities, who get to display publicly on the reality occluding and defining screens, are the idols of *homo spectaculum*. Under the conditions of late industrial capitalism, we find those professions that are oriented toward public display are being stripped of personally expressive faculties. Life becomes scripted display; *homo spectaculum*, like typical movie actors, use their rhetorical skills to display themselves as a character. As with the regents of the feudal public sphere, their role is to behave as though they deserve the role given them—so as not to challenge the legitimacy of their power. Thus, politicians, elected to opine, critique and express, find that when they assume their positions of power they are asked to work to systemically generated scripts, rather than act and express. The crucial point is that the role and purpose of action are defined and scripted prior to the action situation.

The fact that, as "celebrities", *homo spectaculum* do not display a unique, real and consistent identity does not undermine their worthiness for acclaim in the age of the spectacle. The fact that they hold the public's eye, that they get to be seen, is enough to render them idols[11]. This description of the role and status of celebrities brings us to a fine distinction that differentiates the instrumental and spectacular societies. Discussing the role of expressive performance in the modern era, Arendt saw that

> the position of action and speech in modern societies is implied when Adam Smith classifies all occupations which rest essentially on performance—such as the military profession, 'churchmen, lawyers, physicians and opera singers' together with 'menial services'. The lowest and most unproductive 'labour'—it was precisely these occupations—healing, flute playing, play-acting—which furnished ancient thinking with examples for the highest and greatest activities of man. (Arendt 1958, p. 207)

Here we see a marked difference from the position of action and speech in the society of *homo spectaculum*. In contemporary society those occupations that rely upon performance—"churchmen, lawyers, physicians and opera singers" along with screen actors, sport stars, directors, politicians—are among the most celebrated and well paid. Adam Smith understood that the end point of instrumentality is that all public value should be determined by its contribution to production. What has changed since then is that the very act of being public has become the rarest (and subsequently, the most valuable) commodity in the society of *homo spectaculum*. Because screens everywhere obscure *homo spectaculum's* reality, what appears on those screens automatically becomes reality defining. Celebrities, therefore, who are seen more often by more people, receive the highest acclaim in the society of *homo spectaculum*, despite the fact they personally produce very little.

Conclusion: *Homo Spectaculum* and the Society of the Spectacle

The preoccupation of the agonistic drive of *homo spectaculum* within private and strategically arranged contexts is the condition of existence of the society of the spectacle. While the public realm of *homo faber* is uncritical because it presents reason as a totality that is beyond criticism, the "public" realm of *homo spectaculum* is uncritical because it occludes real publicity altogether. Whilst *homo faber* instrumentally defines reality, *homo spectaculum* engages with private display in order to prevent a truly public reality from appearing at all.

Habermas, through his depiction of the fragmentation of consciousness, identifies that this is a means for keeping individuals productive. As discussed earlier, after the dominance of instrumentality had served its purpose by stimulating production to eliminate want, capital had to come up with new ways to generate wants and continue to stimulate production. Instrumentalism may have been exhausted in this context, but the instrumental dominance of the public realm meant that unfulfilled agonism was a readily exploitable way to generate further production and consumption.

It is by controlling public space, by infiltrating the lifeworld in which agonism may be strategically manipulated, that those with performative roles essentially function as the channels of cultural transmission that facilitate this colonisation of the lifeworld. Within the world of *homo spectaculum*, publicity is the source of power. *Homo faber* had already discovered that the productive potential of humans was best extracted by establishing work as a kind of reality defining public. The age of the spectacle emerged from the awareness that peoples' productive potential is maximised if every space they engage with is a reality defining space. Because none of these spaces can lay claim to having complete public integrity, ideology becomes fractured, and so does the individual. This allows fragmented individuals to retain their productivity regardless of the conflicts they experience between system and lifeworld. In a sense, the society of *homo spectaculum* signals the complete occlusion of the lifeworld by a continuous series of meaning providing subsystems.

As a result of the usurpation of public reason by rationality, and the subsequent decline of rationality as an ideological totality, the agonistic drive of *homo spectaculum* is engaged by and in various spaces that seek to constitute themselves as meaning givers. Everywhere we go we are given an opportunity to express ourselves—through what we wear, what we do, what we learn and where we live. We always find ourselves in a public space willing to present a reality that is viscerally engaging and satisfies our desire. This does not necessarily lead to a desire for this "public" to present some true reality, as all realities encountered by *homo spectaculum* are virtual. As Habermas identifies, under these conditions the desire for a coherent and consistent identity is undermined, as there is no space for this identity to appear as it really is. The question "who are you really and what do you really believe in?" will not be asked in any earnest way but only to determine how these presumptions and desires might be made functional within the space they inhabit. This is the rise of a new form of control and a new mandate for citizenship: personal sovereignty as the ability to change a personal environment according to shifts in flows of desire.

Homo faber devised a system of mirrors and lenses through which to apprehend reality; in doing so *homo faber* started to produce reality. The production of reality now requires smoke and mirrors as the spectacle obfuscates its connection with productive, material reality and reasserts the gratification of self in its place. What has happened with the society of *homo spectaculum* is that desire is now stimulated so that production can never be satisfied. We are left in a society dominated by instruments we have been fooled into needing.

So here we see the subtle difference between "one dimensional" society as Marcuse describes it, and the emergence of the age of the spectacle. Basically, the age of the spectacle can be seen as the cultural manifestation of "One Dimensional Man"—what happens following the occlusion of the political by the social, or the systemic colonisation of the lifeworld. It can be seen to refer to the obliteration of truly public forums and their usurpation by private interests and the change in subjectivity which results from this. As I shall now describe, the evidence of this change can be witnessed in the move from suburbia to gated communities, from broadcast to narrowcast media, from the town square to the mall, from advertising to branding, and in the move from detached experts to appropriated experts. In each of these cases the change in subjectivity is one that can be reflected as a development from *animal laborans* and *homo faber* to *homo spectaculum*. The useful public realm is superseded by the strategically designed public realm as a realm of personal engagement and expression. We are no longer shaped into instruments, we are shaped into spectacles.

CHAPTER FIVE

The "Public" Realms of Spectacular Society

...As I was walking, I saw a sign there
And on that sign said, NO TRESPASSING
But on the other side, it didn't say nothing
Now, that side was made for you and me.

In the squares of the city - In the shadow of the steeple
By the relief office - I see my people
And some are grumbling and some are wondering
If this land's still made for you and me.

—Woody Guthrie 'This Land is Your Land' (1940)

There is no better way to understand the emergence of *homo spectaculum* than to look at what has happened to public space and those social institutions that seek to provide meaning in late industrial democracies. In this chapter I intend to outline the conditions of the public sphere in the age of the spectacle, and also to highlight how the detachment of systems from the lifeworld has led to a perversion of the public realm beyond that produced by instrumental rationality. In order to approach the issue of how agonism is usurped in late capitalist societies, I will indicate how the control of steering media translates to the control of discursive spaces, which in turn leads to political power. I hope to outline what I mean by suggesting that the public realm of *homo faber* has become further corrupted by the whims of *homo spectaculum*; detailing how the loss of a shared identity forming public has resulted in a change in the expectations associated with publicness.

The first step in this investigation is to analyse the ways that private interests have infiltrated what otherwise might be critical public spaces. This phenomenon has already been introduced as Habermas's refeudalisation of the public sphere and Arendt's occlusion of the public sphere by the social sphere. This infiltration of public spaces takes place as a result of public power being in the hands of essentially private interests.

The common occurrence in the society of *homo spectaculum* is one wherein publicity holds the normative benefits of appearing as public truth without actually having to conform to the public criticism that would allow for real endorsement of that claim—similar to the role of publicity in the feudal era. This kind of publicity is the medium of the society of *homo spectaculum*. We can witness instances of this phenomenon in contemporary versions of public space, in the emergence of branding, and through the employment of cultures of appropriated experts. Through describing the phenomena of the complete strategic colonisation of communicative space, I shall illustrate how each of these spaces harness and placate the agonistic drive *of homo spectaculum*. This serves to identify how the human need for agonism is engaged in order to extract value and productivity from the individual—it shows what *homo spectaculum* surrenders and what the meaning provider gains. While there are some reasons agonistic and deliberative theorists might embrace contemporary changes to the public sphere, these changes also carry hidden threats. Everywhere we find strategic interests pretending to be public, without conforming to the inclusive and responsive procedures that would make such a claim valid.

The Media: From Broadcast to Narrowcast

With the rise of digital technology the traditional role of the mass media as the conduit of the public sphere has been transformed. Rather than media messages originating from one source and being broadcast to many millions in a fairly uniform manner, we now have media messages springing from many millions and being made available simultaneously to many millions. The advantages of such a new media structure are most evident in the shift from a broadcast system of one-to-many to a narrowcast system of many-to-many. However, despite some positive elements, the movement towards more individuated reception presents some severe challenges to the concept of a mediated public sphere.

For the proponents of the hypodermic needle model of media effects the advent of the internet appears to solve a lot of the social problems posed by media influence. The hegemonic and propagandistic elements of mass media are structurally undermined by the internet's horizontal structure. Such a structure bypasses the systems of centralisation and control which theorists such as Adorno and Chomsky have traditionally associated with broadcast media. The basis for this difference is enabled largely by the technology itself. Whereas broadcast media have traditionally shared the limited radiowave frequency, there are no limits to the expansion of digital media; the internet can continue to expand as long as there is the ability to make more memory. Rather than having one oligopoly or central system which might control media messages, the internet therefore allows for the proliferation of diverse media. This structural change in public access to media gave rise to optimism about a new democratic media form, notably from internet enthusiasts such as Howard Rheingold and John Perry Barlow; the latter writing a "Declaration of the Independence of Cyberspace"—so titled to invoke the fervour of the great democratic revolutions—which is worth quoting at length.

> Governments derive their just powers from the consent of the governed. You have neither solicited nor received ours. We did not invite you. You do not know us, nor do you know our world. Cyberspace does not lie within your borders. Do not think that you can build it, as though it were a public construction project. You cannot. It is an act of nature and it grows itself through our collective actions...We are creating a world that all may enter without privilege or prejudice accorded by race, economic power, military force, or station of birth. We are creating a world where anyone, anywhere may express his or her beliefs, no matter how singular, without fear of being coerced into silence or conformity. Your legal concepts of property, expression, identity, movement, and context do not apply to us. They are all based on matter, and there is no matter here. (Barlow 1996)

Just as with the ideal bourgeois sphere the sense of access to power and sovereignty contained within such writings is palpable. However, that the internet presents *such* a separate space also undermines its ability to foster a new public sphere. The move from broadcast to narrowcast media has fostered the development of *homo spectaculum* in a number of ways: through its extensibility; its devaluation of information; and because it came to operate in an already mass media-saturated public sphere.

The primary objection to the internet operating as a medium for public communication is precisely because it contains no singular or real forum where divergent individuals or communities can measure up to one another. Whereas with broadcast media there is a need for people to share the same resource—the radio frequency bandwidth—on the internet people can and will experience the internet according to their pre-existing communities and interests *ad infinitum*. Narrowcast media are no longer a public resource.

Media effects research has responded to the move from broadcast to narrowcast media by emphasising the role that the user plays in simultaneously consuming, constructing and interpreting media messages. In the digital media world, the impact of selective attention and perception is exacerbated by the lack of a shared public forum. Rather than listening to a news broadcast and being exposed to novel and unexpected items, a user of digital media will tend only to find information which they actively seek out.

The result is that media effects research has developed "Cognitive" and "Communication Mediation" models of media effects, which highlight the role the receiver (and their digital community) plays in determining media effects[1]. Such models highlight the circular and isolated process of making meaning in a narrowcast world; this process undermines the position of power the message sender once occupied but also undermines the mediating role which publicity imposes upon communication.

This increasing importance placed on the individual's pre-existing values and beliefs may suggest that we have escaped the threat of "lifeworld colonisation", as money and power play a decreasingly central role in the mediation of public communication[2]. However, there is much evidence to suggest that the use of digital media merely reflects and amplifies mass media messages—a result of using the technology within an already colonised lifeworld. One of the largest current threats to the plurality of the internet is the overwhelming dominance of internet media brands in providing access points to the internet. A raft of mergers between global media giants and companies with a large internet market share (AOL/Time Warner and MSN/NBC being two prominent examples) has ensured that mass media networks can "synergise" with internet content by ensuring passive users are directed towards their most lucrative content. While there is hope that a new generation will be more inclined to more actively use internet media, in 1999 research into internet browsing revealed that 80% of all site visits are to 0.5% of websites (Waxman 2000). This suggests that while the internet may present us with an overwhelming array of media choices, we generally choose to follow the issues which dominate the mass media.

This failure to utilise the communicative possibilities of the internet has been framed is as "The Information Paradox" (Moisy 1997). Broadly stated this refers to the paradoxical relationship between the availability of information and the demand for it—where "the amazing capacity to produce and distribute news...has led to an obvious decrease in consumption" (Moisy 1997, p. 79). While it is possible to understand this decline in interest as a product of simple economics, where excess supply undermines the demand for (and value of) information, it is also sensible to suggest that the declining interest in news and public affairs is a result of Nietzschean *ressentiment*, where, finding the endless amount of information somewhat overwhelming, *homo spectaculum* clings to its pre-existing interests and beliefs with ever greater tenacity. What is evident is that those who use the internet as deliberative theorists hope they might—as a way to critically access and discuss information relating to public issues—are a minority who are typically already well-informed, heavy media users outside of their internet use (Bimber 2000).

Despite these factors the internet certainly undermines the problems of control which have made theorists such as Adorno, Horkheimer, Chomsky and Herman wary of broadcast media. However, instead of generating an entirely new media landscape, it is arguable that the internet extends the power of already existing media giants. Certainly, the internet is more interactive and therefore more expressive than its broadcast predecessor, but it encourages interaction within a detached and privately mediated setting.

Public Space: From Suburbia to Virtual Communities

An associated example of the occlusion of public space by private interests can be seen in the evolution of communities. The development of suburbia has often been criticised for encouraging uniformity and detachment from external influences; and gated communities represent a spectacular manifestation of this one dimensional tendency. The general idea behind gated communities is to group together like-minded and comparably resourced people in the interests of harmony and security (Bickford 2000). Whilst this seems to recreate the preconditions of Habermas's ideal public sphere, in which participants share a common lifeworld and common goals, in essence it is simply changing public space into private space, dominated by private concerns. As Evan McKenzie has noted, the original impetus for the creation of gated communities arose not from a democratic utopian ideal, but derived from an economic rationale; gated communities allow for shared resources and the private development of infrastructure (McKenzie 1994, pp. 80-84). Of course, the defining characteristic of a gated community, which undermines its claim to be an ideal public space, is that it is gated. Such communities exclude for the sake of private interests, rather than include in an effort to establish public interests. The result of this is that any notion of truly inclusive public interest becomes alien to private public spaces.

Gated communities are politically organised on the basis of what is good for property values—this necessitates strategically determined limitations on personal expression, what you may do with your property, and even restrictions on what kind of people may enter the "public" space (McKenzie 1994, pp. 12-18, 147-149). While it constitutes a public space, what this space is missing is the plurality which, according to Arendt's understanding, is necessary for truth to reveal itself. Whether the gated community is rich or poor, it is basically a tool of segregation wherein public space loses its public nature and becomes a haven for collective *ressentiment* as opposed to critical engagement with others (Bickford 2000). By avoiding engagement with the real world, constituted by plurality, gated communities develop a systemic reality which is, in essence, virtual. Virtual communities have become a hallmark of the age of the spectacle, where, deprived of a noble and heroic affirmation of reality and self, *homo spectaculum* clings to its virtual communities in an ever more feverish process of *ressentiment*.

The Internet as Public Space

In search of a replacement for lost shared space, many democratic theorists have recently begun to turn their attention to what they believe to be the utopian possibilities of the internet as public space. Insofar as the internet provides entertainment through virtual engagement, while occluding public space with what is essentially a proliferation of private spaces, the internet is the quintessential public space of *homo spectaculum*. As with gated communities, the internet seeks to cater to individuals' need for publicity in order to satisfy some of the conditions of a public forum. However, when we understand the internet as a public space that functions in the context of the systemic colonisation of the lifeworld, we find that the internet further panders to the detachment from reality that is encouraged by the technology of the spectacle, and is emblematic of the "public" experience of *homo spectaculum*.

The final pieces of public internet infrastructure were bought up by commercial communications companies before the turn of the last century, meaning the claim that the internet is a form of public space is immediately suspect[3], yet it is often depicted as an open public forum. Much of the optimism concerning the internet as a new form of public space relates to its properties as an egalitarian medium for the distribution of information. The internet appears public, from this perspective, because the ability to publish on the internet is open to anyone with access to some space on a server. Insofar as the internet enables its users to simultaneously receive, alter and compose the media that they are engaged with, there has been a suggestion that this space resists the coloniser/colonised dichotomy. As Mark Poster has put it:

> The magic of the internet is that it is a technology that puts cultural acts, symbolizations in all forms, in the hands of all participants; it radically decentralizes the positions of speech, publishing, filmmaking, radio and television broadcasting, in short the apparatuses of cultural production. (Poster 1997, p. 222)

What is important here is the notion that one composes the media at the same time that one absorbs it. Unlike more traditional forms of mass public communication, such as broadcast and print media, the participant in the interaction is an active component in the composition of that media (Poster

1995). Such a perspective presents the possibility that the internet might bring about a new structural transformation of the public sphere, one that manifests a critical and agonistic relationship between self and world.

It is undeniable that the internet—and digital technology—offers up some wonderful opportunities for ideal communication and—as a result—for democracy. The development of internet technology has indicated that greater openness and interactivity will be the aim of internet media for some time to come. For instance, the rise of open-source programming is a movement which embraces all the tenets of ideal communication—it is inclusive, free and relies upon the creative collaboration between diverse and distinct contributors. Similarly, the development of web interfaces has meant that a new generation of internet surfers expect that their media will adapt to their interests and respond to their questions and demands[4]. For these reasons, there are many reasons to be optimistic about the internet's operation as a public sphere.

However, the validity of this optimistic interpretation is undermined by the facile version of interaction with "reality" that the internet offers. From Arendt's perspective, the experience of the world in virtual space is always removed at least one degree from the reception of the senses. While the internet is actually composed of a multitude of servers linked in a network, its representation in the world is via a screen, generally a screen within the private setting of the household or work. This private nature of reception tends to undermine many otherwise public properties that the internet might have. Unlike the salons and coffee houses of the bourgeois public sphere, the proliferation of screens in contemporary "cybercafes" actually inhibits engagement with the visceral public by engaging the user in a virtual reality that is not connected to any physical public[5]. Whereas the salons and coffee houses of the enlightenment compelled people to publicly interact, there is no such compulsion in the society of the spectacle—where cybercafés and smartphones allow people to always be occupied with their private world.

Certainly, the internet provides a far more engaging and reflexive medium than newspapers and broadcast media. However, the internet is so personalised an experience precisely because nothing about it is public. One may move from one privately created space to another, but as one does, nothing about one's identity or reality remains constant. Apart from a few specifically constructed spaces participation on the internet is anonymous, with no compulsory connection between your online identity and your identity in the real world[6]. The lack of coherent identities on the internet undermines its virtue as a "public" space since some of the principal purposes of public space are to allow identity to reveal itself and to create a space for recognition of self. The internet does not force us to gain a perspective on reality through plurality but rather panders to our preconceived tastes and habitual choices. What we find, then, is that, in essence, the removal of public space from a real community removes the individual from direct participation in that community and those encounters with "the other" that this participation entails (Wilson 1997, p. 159). The virtual reality of the online world creates an escape from the reality of community, and re-establishes community as something ephemeral rather than compelling. The internet only allows the development of character, reputation and identity within the confines of a controlled digital space. Whilst this can lead individuals to form the impression that they are engaged with the media, the falsity of such an impression is evident from the facile relationship this feeling of engagement has with reality. As with all "public" spaces of *homo spectaculum*, personal engagement is represented but is not necessarily connected to public action.

Social networking sites present an interesting test case of how identity online relates to the real world. Such sites thrive upon the establishment of identity and the formation of communities through which expressive agonism can be engaged. For these reasons, one may look upon social networking sites as a profound opportunity to re-engage with public space in a way that facilitates direct and expressive participation in public affairs. Such technology could be used to open up debates to all individuals, re-engaging them in the critical process of making public decisions. Of course, there are a number of reasons this is unlikely to happen. Firstly, according to Arendt's schemata, social networking sites are an instance of social space, rather than public space. The difference is that social space is essentially private space made public, whereas ideally, public space is a place for the debate of public issues. If private space is made public, it loses its ability to emerge from a private setting and, with it, its ability to contribute something unique or revelatory to a public (Arendt 1958, pp. 56–71). Social networking sites present the possibility that our activity is watched at all times, and with this comes the very real possibility that people will never act, but rather behave, as they know they are under constant surveillance. Finally, social networking sites are not conducive to public space because they are privately owned and run for profit. The result of this is that behaviour is monitored and regulated in order to stimulate profitable behaviour; furthermore, the content of social networking sites remains the property of social networking sites, so that one's creative expression can actually be appropriated for the private profit of the site owner.

The basis of criticisms of the influence of information and communications technology on the public sphere is that it places an instrument of systemic influence—a screen—between self and the lifeworld. Although the textual content of internet discussion is subjectively constituted, the forum through which that text is exchanged is not. It appears public, it entertains notions of publicity, it is intended to appear public and provides some of the functions of a public; but essentially it is governed by non-linguistic steering media, of which money and power are pre-eminent.

Screens emulate public space because if they don't they must compete with public space. For it is by serving the functional purposes of public space that the screen occludes the need for truly public space; by suppressing this need, which otherwise might demand satisfaction. Thus, the internet undermines the existence of a real public by providing effects like those that might otherwise be derived from an actual public. Nowhere is this more evident than in the rise of social networking sites, which thrive upon their appearance as a well-attended public space.

Simon Cooper encapsulates this process of occlusion in a discussion of the political implications of "virtual reality":

> Consistently in the discourse of VR there is a tendency to devalue the variety of concrete social and environmental settings that gives meaning to human activity. The assumption of autonomy, of the subject's freedom to create comes only through removing the subject from these settings. The promise of a mode of being which takes place on this abstracted level ends up enforcing a process of reification rather than resisting or overcoming it. The fundamental alienation that VR offers severs the subject from the very possibility of experiences which might be more resistant to the process of commodification that s/he is partly trying to escape. (Cooper 1997, pp. 102–103)

Here we see how the insertion of a technological mediator in communication can automatically disengage the critical process of the interaction between identity and "reality". Through its presentation of virtual realities as being as valid or validating as offline reality itself, the internet can be seen as pacifying our search for what is "real".

Hence, while the internet may broaden our scope of experience, it does not make that experience any more real. As Michelle Wilson has pointed out, the experience of assuming an identity online provides some insight into people's reactions and behaviour online but it is by no means the same as the embodied experience in the real world (Wilson 1997, p. 149). It can be argued that the ephemeral quality of the internet undermines the very possibility of purposeful action. The internet as public space offers a peculiarly detached experience, and this detachment, while seemingly engaging, can be seen to produce facile experiences precisely because it has no connection with the limitations and constraints of the real world. As Jean-Pierre Dupuy notes, "a world without constraints, without order, a world in which everything would be possible, would have no meaning" (Dupuy 1980, p. 13).

> Virtual community is the illusion of community where there are no real people and no real communication. It is a term used by idealistic technophiles who fail to understand that authentic community cannot be engendered through technological means. (Wilbur 1997, p. 14)

Without a tangible and personal commitment to care about the integrity of a public, virtual publics tend to lack the structure and conditions necessary to approximate ideal speech.

In its manifestation as a screen the internet co-opts its users by catering to their "public" needs while surreptitiously seeking to govern such needs[7]. Whilst the potentials of the internet as a public sphere are certainly exciting[8], the actual status of the internet as a public sphere in the current political climate reflects the condition in which private strategic interests come to occlude what otherwise might be communicative spaces. The idea that the internet can be thought of as a public sphere, despite the fact that it is fundamentally privately owned and privately experienced, is a symptom of the fact that *homo spectaculum* has no reference points which would allow us to recognise a *real* public.

The Market: From Commons to Commodities

Arendt is a vocal proponent of the value of private space as a place to develop one's uniqueness. However, she also argues that the desire to develop uniqueness has to be generated through the individual's engagement with an expressive and plural public. If one were to search for the nearest thing to the agonistic meeting place of a Greek polis in contemporary liberal democracies the first port of call would be the shopping centre. It is here that *homo spectaculum* is encouraged to engage in the activities of expressing, discussing and deciding that Arendt recognises as the activities of human freedom (Arendt 1990, p. 235). This freedom is confined by a crossroads of commerce[9], through which the public pass while conducting their business. It is the closest thing to what would be regarded in English towns as "the common", or what in Spain would be "the plaza". The fact that shopping centres have replaced the village green is a function of instrumental rationality—there is a greater quantifiable utility in the constant use of public space for commerce. The ways in which this occlusion of public space affects individual perceptions of reality, however, is more a function of the subsequent colonisation of the lifeworld. As a direct result of being "common" the shopping centre becomes a centre of agonistic engagement; a place where values are debated and instilled. To see how this instillation takes place, it pays to remember Habermas's formulation of lifeworld colonisation occurring through systemic influence on areas of cultural transmission.

If we accept the fact that shopping centres occupy the role of the modern "commons", it is not hard to extrapolate from this that they therefore have an effect on the transmission of culture[10]. Young adults "hang out" at the shopping centre because it is an accessible place, as they might once have met on the commons or in the plaza. They meet to engage with each other and to participate in their culture. Adults, intentionally or not, also receive impressions about "reality" from their experiences in shopping centres. Of course "public" spaces like these are not public at all, but are pervaded by an association of private interests that seek to strategically manipulate the "public" forum, to make certain behaviour unproblematic.

Some powerful examples of why shopping centres are not true public space can be found in security policies that prohibit beggars and buskers, pamphleteers and political dissidents from disrupting the flow of commerce. A study of the legal parameters for political action in United States shopping malls indicates that, while democratic rights to free speech are occasionally upheld due to the "public" nature of malls, the majority of cases concerning restrictions of free speech in malls are dismissed because shopping malls are private property (Kohn 2001). Private property, it is argued, "does not lose its private character merely because the public is generally invited to use it for designated purposes" (Kohn 2001, p. 74). As a result, the private owners are permitted to prohibit unprofitable, or even unwanted, "expressive conduct" within their shopping malls.

So here we see how the public forums of *homo spectaculum* in some ways emulate Arendt's formulation of the public realm of *animal laborans*. That is, a public space distinguished by the absence of speech and action. This prohibition of public criticism is reminiscent of Arendt's account of the initial bourgeois claim on political power. "Society", she claims, "assumed the disguise of an organization of property owners who, instead of claiming access to the public realm because of their wealth, demanded protection from it for the accumulation of more wealth" (Arendt 1958, p. 68). Insofar as they *contain* the public space as a way of stifling critical expression, the property owners of the contemporary shopping centre recreate the public realm of *animal laborans*—mute and uncritical.

However, the public realms of *homo spectaculum* also share *homo faber's* public purpose of creating meaning. Naomi Klein develops the argument that while curtailing criticism is a fortuitous by-product of the benefits of property ownership, the real reason that shop owners like malls is because malls allow them to fabricate and cultivate a consumer culture (Klein 2000). The shopping mall can be a place of silence and sterility, but it rarely is. More often the shopping mall is dominated by expression and spectacle—but specifically that expression deemed to suit the interests of the property owners. Hence we find the shopping mall is, at least to some extent, a manifestation of the public realm designed by *homo faber*. It is humans as instrumentalisers who fabricate shopping malls and it is they who dictate the cultural transmission they deem necessary. To this end they create a culture that depends upon the agonistic interaction they offer within their fabricated world.

As with employers who understand that the best way to get the most out of their employees is to validate their expressive conduct and channel it towards the purposes of their enterprise, the shopping centre validates the person who makes purchases. Consumption is the only allowable way to effectively display in a shopping centre—and incentives such as rewards programs, cross-promotions and personally validating service are available to those who "buy in". Thus we see how the public realms of *homo spectaculum* share the characteristics of those of *animal laborans* and *homo faber*. On the one hand, shop owners engage individuals within a "public" they define; on the other hand, they channel this engagement into furthering their own private and strategic interests, undermining the communicative role that publics would otherwise serve.

Before turning to a discussion of the ways in which private interests engage the agonism of citizens in the market, it is important to understand this use of space within the context of the role that publicity plays in cultural transmission. When a community of shop owners decides to redevelop as a mall they do so essentially because it gives them control over that environment; not only control over critical voices, as just mentioned, but also control over the temperature, cleanliness and presentation of that world. They essentially create a pseudo-public space—akin to a screen—which is regulated and designed with their interests in mind. This does not stop it from being a "public" place for those who go there and indeed, as suggested earlier, they like to encourage this notion of publicity by catering to "public" needs. Their interest in publicity is, however, in no way earnest. Public space is one of the

> areas of action that resist being converted over to the media of money and power because they are specialized in cultural transmission, social integration and child rearing, and remain dependent on mutual understanding as a mechanism for coordinating action. (Habermas 1987b, p. 330)

What the fabricators of shopping centres are hoping to exploit is this dependence on mutual understanding which, following the uncoupling of the system from the lifeworld, is the wellspring of competitive engagement. Thus, they seek to fabricate a world of spectacular values which they can imbue in their public, and reap the subsequent profits.

A steady stream of critical theorists have identified consumption's role in placating the masses. From Adorno and Horkheimer to Hardt and Negri, the rise of the agonism of the market is seen as evidence of the advanced capitalist system undermining the possibility of revolutionary politics. These theorists argue that capital has developed new ways of containing revolutionary forces and that its chief means of doing so is through engaging the agonism of individuals as consumers. In the face of active engagement with private, corporate and quasi-corporate interests, there is less incentive to engage in political citizenship and a greater incentive to let the business of government proceed without public interest or criticism (Rose 2000, p. 327).

The ability to command such a "public space"—a screen—translates into the ability to establish a projection of reality, and the subsequent ability to become a culturally important identity marker. Arendt saw that in a world where identity is fluid "Men, their ever-changing nature notwithstanding, can retrieve their sameness, that is, their identity, by being related to the same chair and the same table" (Arendt 1958, p. 137). The desire to use products as a source of meaning is ever more demanding in the absence of a meaningfully constructed public. Those who determine the capacities of markets are aware of this and for this reason have devised the phenomenon of branding. The rise and rise of branding within the system of consumption and production is a symptom of the fact that the market has replaced politics as the agonistic theatre *par excellence*.

Advertising: From Editorial Influence to Branding

Branding describes the process of adding value to commodities by giving them social meaning. This has become the primary goal of marketing and represents an attempt by those in the corporate world to command "the most valuable real-estate in the world, a corner of the consumer's mind" ("Building Brands" 2004). Brands have come to colonise the lifeworld as individuals have come to relate to each other and themselves in terms of their material possessions and investments. Companies that used to concentrate on producing products to meet these needs are now focusing on producing brands to meet these needs. In her examination of this process, *No Logo*, Naomi Klein has uncovered the surreptitious occupation of public space and personal engagement by brands (Klein 2000). In a large part of this work Klein investigates the colonisation of public space by private interests, but her main point is that the intent of private interests in usurping this public space is to become normative governors, "chief communicators of all that is good and cherished in our culture" (Klein 2000, p. 335).

In seeking to occupy a position of greater importance than the use value of their actual product, brand owners are trying to cash in on their position as meaning providers, not product providers. As Phil Knight declared in his role as the chief executive officer of a footwear company:

> For years we thought of ourselves as a production-oriented company, meaning we put all our emphasis on designing and manufacturing the product. But now we understand that the most important thing we do is market the product.[11]

Marketers understand the value of maintaining the role of meaning providers as a means to increase profit. As Klein describes it, the process of branding involves developing meaningful normative constructions that are marketable to consumers—this moves the role of the corporation from producing the product to producing the product's meaning. Hence IBM does not sell computers, it sells business solutions. Levis does not simply sell jeans; it sells a way of life (Klein 2000, pp. 23–24). In this role the market consciously fulfils the role of meaning provider through its control over identity forming discursive spaces. The way marketers do so is once again by usurping public spaces, which are areas of cultural transmission, in order to have an undue effect on action coordination. As Hardt and Nergri described it in *Empire*: "Capitalism sets in motion a continuous cycle of private reappropriation of public goods: The expropriation of what is common" (Hardt & Negri 2000, p. 301).

The most notable and obvious forms of the intrusion of the market into cultural transmission are through markets intertwining with the media. However, far beyond the practice of censoring content, which for Habermas began with the advent of the penny press, market forces now seek to saturate the private worlds of individuals in such a way that they come to constitute culture itself[12]. The challenge of marketers seeking to brand effectively is to relate meaningfully to their target markets and occupying positions of public importance is integral to fulfilling this role[13]. By infiltrating the lifeworld, or occluding it, marketers appear communicative while actually pursuing strategic aims.

In order to fulfil the role of meaning givers, marketers have had to play the role of philosophers. They become the "organs of the Zeitgeist" (Arendt 1958, p. 294), divining the good life and selling it. As a result marketers now do research into what people think, not necessarily to find out what they think about a product and how to improve it, but rather to find out which shared preconceptions of their lifeworld are likely to motivate them to purchase a product. It is the market that seeks to engage and thematise the important issues of the public world in order to gain the emotional leverage needed to motivate individuals to buy. Hence, the role of the consumer expert has changed from data analysis and prediction to exploring concepts of validity through cultural studies, ethnographies and personal introspection (Wehner 2001).

As a result advertising has become creative, poetic and in many senses political[14]. Advertising involves making value statements, redeeming claims to truth and appealing to the capacity for understanding within the target audience. When the workers of the society of the spectacle finish their dehumanising labour, they find at home in their private space "they are treated like grown-ups, with a great show of solicitude and politeness, in their new role as consumers" (Debord 1995, p. 30). Brands are created in an effort to rhetorically engage the public. They are developed to "establish emotional ties" with their customers so that the brand might "[weave] itself into the fabric of people's lives", providing a basis of reality and an opportunity for "emotional leverage"[15]. For this reason, marketers seeking to brand are amongst the most fervent miners of lifeworld understandings, and do so in order to make their claims to legitimacy valid.

The brand rationality has penetrated areas of cultural transmission, including child rearing: shoe manufacturers run anti-bullying campaigns in schools and department stores teach children how to shop for themselves (Monbiot 2001). Klein cites a specific example of a child being suspended from school "for wearing a Pepsi shirt on Coke day" (Klein 2000, p. 95), an incident which is Orwellian in terms of its level of political control. Klein also cites the case of an American elementary school maths book which "was riddled with mentions and photographs of well known brand name products: Nike shoes, McDonald's, Gatorade" which was defended on the basis that "you're trying to get into what people are familiar with, so that they can see, hey, mathematics is in the world out there"[16]. Through their infiltration of areas of cultural transmission commodities come to constitute the world— commodities are presented as immortal as the reason contained within mathematics. Thus, in a manner that reflects Arendt's description of the public realm of *homo faber*, the contemporary world of things comes to be the basic foundation of all other relations between humans. By colonising the lifeworld, through occluding what should be political space with the social, private interests commandeer publicity for their own ends.

Once again, it pays to consider how the lifeworld itself is colonised through systemic rationality entering into areas of cultural transmission. The control of media through advertising, and the control of public space through privatisation are obvious ways to access processes of cultural transmission and become meaning providers, but these are not the only way to do so. As Klein points out, the tendency towards multinational and multimedia mergers have allowed brands to invade every aspect of modern life. Brands are cultural commanders. Their political power is witnessed in the way their language infiltrates the everyday exchanges of the lifeworld, which in turn gives them an ability to constitute reality. Microsoft spellcheckers will recognise "Coca Cola", but not "reification"; it has "Subaru" in its dictionary, but not "commodification", this is the reality of discursive control. In actuality, branding appears to be the most recent incarnation of reification, the act of regarding an abstract phenomenon as a material thing. Branding appeals to the individual's need for an identity forming context, for a meaningful reality to relate to. It is a process employed in the public realm of *homo spectaculum*, because such a public realm has an excess of material goods and a dearth of *real* meaning.

Public Expertise: From Appropriating Experts to Isolating Experts

Habermas contends that the everyday language of the lifeworld is the most powerful critical tool available to those seeking to address the colonisation of the lifeworld—the use of a shared vocabulary enables truth claims to be easily redeemed and reasonable argumentation to take place. The development of expert cultures is the antithesis of this situation, as cultures of expertise operate within their own domains of legitimacy secured according to systemic imperatives. As Marx predicted, this specialisation has the immediate effect of alienating experts from their own humanity, their own lifeworld (Marx 1990, pp. 481–482). The development of systems of experts not only serves to stifle critical input from the lifeworld, it inhibits inter-systemic criticism and the development of holistic approaches to overarching social problems. As Hardt and Negri point out, "The neutralization of the transcendental imagination is thus the first sense in which the political in the imperial domain is ontological" (Hardt & Negri 2000, p. 354). The current state of thought is one in which knowledge within a system is valued, as opposed to admiring general propensities for reason and wisdom. Functional knowledge in the world of *homo spectaculum* is knowledge at the level of the screen, not of the reality that lies behind it.

The political nature of ontology can be further explained in terms of the way in which the role of public expertise has been privatised. In light of the previous discussion, one of the most obvious examples of the privatisation of experts can be witnessed as one of the facets of branding. In attempting to sell products, private interests often present "expert" opinions that validate their claims to truth. The use of this device has become prolific and, as identified by Naomi Wolf in *The Beauty Myth*, some of the best examples can be found in the beauty industry (Wolf 1991). In what is a seminal text on the function of branding, Wolf identifies the ways in which expertise is either simply purchased, or otherwise simulated, in order to endorse a product and an image. The power of the "expert" arises from the legitimacy of apparently public institutions endorsing private claims. The pseudo-scientific posturing of the beauty industry raises questions such as: exactly what kind of qualifications does one need in order to graduate from the "Ponds Institute"[17]? The private command over steering media, the money to purchase expertise (along with the concurrent condition that experts allow themselves to be bought rather than defend the integrity of their character and research) or the power to imitate the spectacle of expertise, are forms of the commodification of knowledge.

Indeed, the corruption of expertise is further engaged in the society of *homo spectaculum*, in which appearance is more important than substance. For the manipulation of expertise by those with access to "public" forums is endemic. This can happen as a result of the use of steering media to "buy out" expertise, or through the abuse of control over a "public" that essentially has no critical mechanisms that cannot be purchased. An excellent example of this is identified by Klein, who describes how the dominant English pharmaceutical brand Boots commissioned a study to compare thyroid drugs and then withdrew the rights to publication when a competitor tested in the study was found to be superior to, and cheaper than, Boots' product (Klein 2000). Another example of the abuse of "public credentials" was uncovered by journalist George Monbiot who found that Monsanto, the agricultural production company, not only attempted to buy out critical experts, but also falsely created its own experts to publicly deride an article that was critical of their products and practices, causing the unprecedented retraction of the critical article (Monbiot 2002). This case was particularly insidious, as Monsanto was found to have presented false identities as "experts" on an internet forum in order to generate a petition against the critical article. It did not matter that these experts did not really exist, their protests were spectacular enough to be treated as authentic. Monbiot points out that the development of massive and coherent private interests comes to dominate the public sphere by dominating every facet of publicity. Quite simply, in lieu of a truly public place to expose the truth, private interests run riot.

Academia has not been immune to the appropriation of expertise. This can be seen in systemic influence over the kind of expertise that has developed under the conditions of late capitalism and it can also be witnessed in the postmodern attitude towards critical theory. As an instance of the first order, one only need witness the incredible growth and dominance of business schools in most contemporary academic institutions. As lamented by John Ralston Saul, this development reflects academia's changed purpose from fostering critical thinkers to generating foot soldiers for the new economy; a direct consequence of the historical dominance of the public realm by *homo faber* (Ralston Saul 1997, p. 127). Beyond the dominance of utility in public institutions we witness the emergence of branded knowledge; with the proliferation of corporate teaching material, courses and educational programs. Through the process of creating its own privately determined "public" knowledge "business stands as a guard dog at the gates of perception"[18]. In the society of *homo spectaculum* universities help to ensure the continuity of screens. The places of thought are everywhere replaced by places of knowledge and, once again, private interests establish the boundaries, purpose and utility of knowledge.

Finally, those areas of academia that remain devoted to critical thought have themselves been somewhat hamstrung by the development of postmodern thinking. The postmodern approach to knowledge is perfectly suited to the world of screens, with the development of fetishistic specialisations and the dissolution of reality in a way that validates the continual reinvention of meaning; it is the best possible functional language for areas such as marketing and management in the information economy (Hardt & Negri 2000, pp. 151–152, 159). As mentioned above, those areas of academia that specialise in the relationship of the system to the lifeworld and in the methods of cultural reproduction have been appropriated by the marketers. In the public realm dominated by the values of *homo faber*, novel theoretical insight into what drives the minds of consumers is invaluable market research. Meanwhile the possibility for a transcendental and unifying critical theory is undermined by the postmodern approach, which leads to the view that theories of change are self-defeating and misguided. Postmodernism, the theory that reality itself is a construct, undermines the plausibility that there is a reality behind the screen, and thus allows the screen to be taken as reality.

The Public Role of Spectacles

The problem that Arendt and Habermas would have with the society dominated by *homo spectaculum* is that there is no critical depth to any of its spaces. This is despite the fact that elements of the society of *homo spectaculum*—such as incredulity towards instrumentality, the development of egalitarian communication structures and personally responsive technologies—seem to hold much promise for a critical and engaged democratic polis.

Market forces certainly promote communication between vendors and consumers, in which marketers and interactive technologies mine the shared assumptions of lifeworlds in order to position their products in such a way as to make them appealing. As the advertising industry's own experts assure us, the marketers' only interest is in effective product distribution, in giving the people what they want (Sutherland 1993, pp. 96-98). Indeed, as prominent Habermasian Thomas McCarthy has noted, the market itself could be used as an excellent example of how a system can be oriented towards reaching understanding (McCarthy 1985, p. 34). After all, the market does not discriminate, it brings people together and it seeks to understand the needs and motivations of its consumers. After describing the ways in which the market functionally resembles an ideal speaking situation, McCarthy makes the point that, while claims that the market is an "ideal" forum may be spurious, they remain more plausible than the claim that any modern democracy is norm-free, ethically neutral and functionally responsive (McCarthy 1985, p. 34). If advertising companies fulfil the role of philosophers, at least philosophy is taking place. Indeed, the organic intellectuals of capital are devising new ways to explore the political sensibilies of its subjects; they engage, question and respond far more effectively than the ossifying political system of *homo faber*. Furthermore, with the rise of personally enabling technologies, the market has extended the capacity of agents to affect the world. Thus the development of digital technologies is the latest stage in a technological process that results in the individual's seamless integration with capital. While the market responds, the political system of *homo faber* becomes a ludicrous parody of its decaying and forgotten essence. Following the rise of the society of *homo spectaculum*, and the consequent capture of the agonistic and subsequently political drives of the individual by the market, the really pertinent issue concerns whether anyone is able to care that the political, as Arendt identified it, has been occluded.

In order to respond to this challenge, it is important to understand that what prevents the market of the society of *homo spectaculum* from being or becoming the political theatre *par excellence* is the lack of the true and earnest publicness that would make the manifestations of the current public realm "real"[19]. The market is not a value free meeting place of ideas and it does not simply respond to consumer's demands. The market has assumed a position of publicity despite the fact that it is not truly public; it represents private interests, and does so in such a way that some private interests are represented more effectively than others. The market does engage the agonistic drive of what otherwise might be political citizens, but it does not do so in the earnest and communicative fashion required by agonistic and deliberative democrats. Rather, it is a complex series of systems in which legitimacy is based directly upon the distribution of money and power. There is no obligation for participants in the market to care for others (at least in a manner that might make market activity communicative), and if instrumentally mining the lifeworld of its riches will strip that lifeworld of its sacredness, there is no mechanism in the market to prevent it from doing so. Finally, the market cannot be made publicly accountable and does not approach anything like the inclusive and engaging democratic processes that it would need to embrace in order to meet deliberative and agonistic requirements for democracy. The market may possess progressive features, it has certainly encouraged and enabled the rationalisation of the lifeworld; however, because it cannot reconcile identity with reality, it does not possess the qualities of an ideal public space as is understood by Habermas and Arendt.

As with all the "public" realms of *homo spectaculum*, these screens serve to engage and satisfy the individual's agonistic drive in such a way as to occlude the need for a real public space. So, much of the virtue of public participation arises from the fact that public interaction is what provides a sense of the "real". Without a common and immanent public space in which to come to understand what is real, humans are left isolated and disempowered, and vulnerable to the *ressentiment* that the social sphere provides. By removing the construction of self from the world of real experience, these screens can be seen as undermining the critical potential of public space by extending the lifeworld to such an extent that there can be no critical depth to any of it. Here we come in contact with a criticism that Arendt makes of the banality of evil:

> It is indeed my opinion now that evil is never 'radical', that it is only extreme, and that it possesses neither depth nor any demonic dimension. It can overgrow and lay waste the whole world precisely because it spreads like a fungus on the surface. It is 'thought-defying,' as I said, because thought tries to reach some depth, to go to the roots, and the moment it concerns itself with evil, it is frustrated because there is nothing. That is its 'banality'. Only the good has depth and can be radical. (Arendt 1978a, pp. 250–251)

In the flatness of the screen we witness the one dimensional origins of the society of *homo spectaculum* and the threat that the screens of *homo spectaculum* pose to human subjectivity. For these screens extend over everything, seemingly constituting a public which, precisely because of its lack of depth and real immanence, can never truly be public.

PART THREE

SPECTACULAR ®EVOLUTION: DEMOCRACY AND THE SPECTACLE

The Politics of the Spectacle

> Every age has its massive moral blindspots.
> We might not see them, but our children will.
>
> —Bono (2004)

The emergence of *homo spectaculum* results in a complete misfiring of the critical imperatives of the democratic system. While we still have a political public realm created by *homo faber*, society itself has become dominated not by a universal rationality but by a series of fragmented systems which, as a totality, occlude opportunities for truly public engagement. This is a result of the infestation of public space by a myriad of private interests, the development of a new impetus for (re)production and the fragmentation of subjectivity that results. The political system has remained focused on catering to the political demands of *homo faber* and *animal laborans*—keeping citizens safe and productive. Meanwhile, markets have generated new and ingenious ways to cater to consumers' agonistic desire. By channelling the frustrated desire of contemporary citizens to display towards private ends, those who strategically control discursive spaces usurp citizens' desire to critically engage with political decisions.

The political institutions of *homo faber* remain organised on the basis of the old liberal conception of the individual; however, following the structural transformation of the public sphere, these same institutions deny the opportunity for public expression to the individual.

> The establishment of basic political rights in the framework of mass democracy means, on one hand, a universalization of the role of citizen and, on the other hand, a segmenting of this role from the decision making process, a cleansing of political participation from any participatory content. (Habermas 1987b, p. 250)

Insofar as citizens' agonism is actually engaged in the "private" spaces they inhabit in an immediate, gratifying and functional way, the system of representative voting on "public" issues every four years becomes rather obsolete as an agonistic engagement.

In the society of *homo spectaculum*

> citizenship is not primarily realised in a relation with the state, nor does it involve
> participation in a uniform public sphere; citizenship, rather, entails active engagement
> in a diversified and dispersed variety of private, corporate and quasi-corporate
> practices, of which working and shopping are paradigmatic. (Rose 2000, p. 327)

Whilst the state seeks to compete with the market by addressing citizens as consumers, it fails to foster the critical, expressive role that Habermas and Arendt believe is integral to a virtuous public space. The market has responded to the citizen's need for agonistic engagement, whereas the political system remains unresponsive and devoid of plural criticism. In the context of a world pervaded by screens, the political system of representative liberal democracies shrinks, for the most part, to a relatively derivative subsystem of power distribution.

While the political symptom of the public realm dominated by *homo faber* was an exclusion of critical voices that could not phrase their arguments in terms of instrumental rationality, the political symptom of *homo spectaculum* is a complete lack of association between the public realm of *homo faber* and meaningful political expression. Whilst *homo faber* does not care about anything that wasn't quantifiable, *homo spectaculum* is motivated to care about more than pure instrumentality, but does not identify the political system of *homo faber* as a meaningful place to do so as, quite simply, there is no space for political action. In their private world, at work and when consuming *homo spectaculum* is continually reminded that every decision they make says something about them. But when it comes to politics, their only meaningful participation is to enter a small, bland booth alone, and secretly make a meaningless choice.

The Blurring of Public and Private Spaces

This shift of meaning defining contexts into the private realm has undermined the quality of private space as Arendt understands it. For Arendt, the quality of the public realm depends upon its detachment from the private realm.

> While [entirely public life] retains its visibility, it loses the quality of rising into sight
> from some darker ground which must remain hidden if it is not to lose its depth in a
> very real non-subjective strength…The only efficient way to guarantee the darkness of
> what needs to be hidden against the light of publicity is private property, a privately
> owned place to hide in. (Arendt 1958, p. 71)

The proliferation of screens and meaning providers in private contexts makes it very hard for *homo spectaculum* to judge exactly what is private and what is public. Under this condition, the boundary between the real world and the constructed world is fractured; and the distinction between public and private becomes completely blurred.

> The spectacle erases the dividing line between self and world, in that the self, under siege by the presence/absence of the world, is eventually overwhelmed: it likewise erases the dividing line between true and false, repressing all directly lived truth beneath the real presence of the falsehood maintained by the organisation of appearances. The individual, though condemned to the passive acceptance of an everyday reality, is thus driven into a form of madness in which, by resorting to magical devices, he entertains the illusion that he is reacting to his fate. The recognition and consumption of commodities are at the core of this pseudo-response to a communication to which no response is possible. The need to imitate that the consumer experiences is indeed a truly infantile need, one determined by every aspect of his fundamental dispossession. (Debord 1990, p. 153)

The dual effect of the proliferation of private spaces that usurp the role of public space is to politicise privacy (affairs of the household) and depoliticise the public (affairs of the common). This is the condition that the market requires in order to remain a meaning giver.

In Habermasian terms, the transfer of world-defining roles to the market means simply that the social constructions shaped by administrative power are undermined while the social constructions shaped by money become more powerful. This is quite a distinct change from the "one dimensional" society dominated by the public realm of *homo faber*, in which all public legitimacy was constrained by a pervasive ideology established through public institutions. The ideologies that dominate public institutions in the "public" realm of *homo spectaculum* are usually generated from the dominant private ideology of the times[1]. Exactly how far the care of *homo spectaculum* extends depends upon the screens she/he is surrounded by. There is nothing rational about this. Command of screens is generally open to those in control of steering media and thus they are the ones who get to manipulate publicity.

Freedom and Steering Media

The concept of spatial control as a form of social control can be seen as being closely related to Habermas's notion of the role of steering media, or money and power. An individual's ability to control money and power determines the extent to which their virtual world reflects their expressions, discussions and decisions. It is not that the working class escapes control, but that their engaging worlds are less real and more likely to be constrained by someone else's expression. While those who have access to steering media can exert some control over the "public" world, those without money and power are more likely to express their agonism within the context defined by those who do. We apportion engagement with the spectacle to everyone. The *real* quality of that engagement becomes the commodifiable element; the greater the control over steering media, the more chance your expression will be effected in the "real" world. Even so, by Arendtian standards, this real world, along with all the "publics" that engage *homo spectaculum*, is not real at all—it is a construction taking the place of reality.

The effect of the interaction of steering media upon private public spaces is that the wealthier you become, the further you can use the steering media to which you have access to assert your particular spectacle as reality. Greater control over money and power translates directly into more control over the screens that exist outside one's immediate area. In current conditions we find that the majority of money and power is concentrated in the hands of very few people. They are not acting together, nor are they necessarily competitive—and they do not necessarily have evil intentions. Yet, those with access to governmental power and news media do not need to ensure the "reality" of what they report. Instead, they are aware that their position in regard to steering media allows them to delineate reality as such, and in such a position they are unlikely to be subjected to critical scrutiny.

On the other hand, the less access people have to money and power, the less "real" or public their reality is likely to be. Those who are deprived of steering media will control only their private environment; possibly their home environment, their work space, perhaps only their bodies. They have less control over the environments in which they make their decisions and therefore control what they can. Insofar as individuals receive their world-orientations passively from the environment, the virtual worlds they inhabit are defined by those who do establish the "public space" in which they engage. The less control people have over steering media, however, the less likely it is that they will have the ability to project their reality as a shared reality; rather they will move within spaces that are projected by others in order to make themselves a functional component of those spaces, without actually being given the power to constitute themselves as an act of unique expression. In the society of *homo spectaculum* the ability to be noble and avoid *ressentiment* is the ability to live according to one's own projection.

The Spectacle and Identity Politics

The dominance of the political realm of *homo faber* in the time of the rise of *homo spectaculum* also contributes to the rise of fundamentalisms, ethnic politics and the extreme detachment of individuals from the instrumental political subsystem. The purpose of public space, as conceived by Habermas and Arendt, is to bring individuals together in a forum that can coordinate public action in a fair and reasonable way, explicitly accepted and constituted by the participants. By failing to encourage the active involvement of citizens in the process of government, the political subsystem has brought about the decline of such a "public" space. The loss of such a space manifests itself as an extreme form of individualism, whereby individuals lose sense of their *real* public identities as a source of value orientation and, instead, seek to locate themselves within an existing set of orientations—opening them up for *ressentiment* in the process[2].

Liberal democracies tend to orient participants through utilitarian notions about private loss and gain, and for this reason state politics is largely redundant as an avenue for political expression in a deliberative or agonistic sense. Thus we find that,

> deprived of the possibility of identifying with valuable conceptions of citizenship, many people are increasingly searching for other forms of collective identification, which can very often put into jeopardy the civic bond that should unite a democratic political association. (Mouffe 2000a, p. 96)

Everywhere citizens abandon the political public space as a space in which they might reasonably and equitably address their political concerns. As a result, they find their outlets of expression in more private forums that are not always conducive to considered or careful thought. The age of the spectacle has thus seen a concurrent rise in levels of extremist identification. Many instances of so-called "terrorism" are only extremely violent outcomes of this process of exclusion; terrorism often appears to be the action of people excluded from proper public participation.

The failure of the public realm of *homo faber* to deal with the political expressiveness of *homo spectaculum* is a direct result of the interaction of the unified political institutions of *homo faber* with the fragmented subjectivity of *homo spectaculum*. Representative liberal democracies, very much based upon the notion of irreducible and consistent individuals, still seek to effect power through discipline over distinct national territories. They operate in this way despite the fact that most citizens' political engagement rarely conforms to that of national territories. The result is that, in attempting to address the concerns of individuals as private citizens, the national governments appropriate public power for private ends, determined through projected "publics" that are not primarily generated by authentically democratic processes.

While the conditions that give rise to *homo spectaculum* are not restricted to national borders, the political apparatus that purports to serve *homo spectaculum* remains fixed to the nation-state. In their function as utilitarian "ends-meeting" government, the role of national governments is to provide the security that the spectacle demands. The reduction of government to the purposes of *homo faber* means that governments fail to cater to the political needs of *homo spectaculum*. Rather, the role of government is confined to finding the solution to technical problems; such as how to secure a supply of oil necessary for continued economic growth or how to avoid international conventions on human rights and resource consumption in order to perpetuate systemic stability. The political subsystem ensures its continued survival by acting as an institutional guarantor of the reality established by those in control of steering media.

In the process, the politics of representative democracies becomes a spectacle, and culture becomes even more spectacular. As we transmit and imbibe the spectacle globally, we continually appropriate wealth and power nationally, and the resulting dissonance between what we expect and what others perceive as legitimate reflects an international conflict between system and lifeworld. Sustained by our national governmental systems we are continually advancing spectacular notions of legitimacy that are not reconcilable with the internationally constituted lifeworld. The conflict that this generates represents the ultimate tension between the spectacular and the real and the resolution of this tension will determine the future human condition. In order to provide further evidence that this subjectivity is emerging, I shall examine some of the practical manifestations of the critical failings of *homo spectaculum*.

The Material Manifestations of the Society of the Spectacle

The Waste Economy

I believe that the most startling cultural aberration caused by the shift of agonistic engagement from the political realm to the market is the thoughtlessness of the waste economy. By encountering our reality as strategically designed by private interests

> we have found a way to act on the earth and within terrestrial nature as though we dispose of it from outside, from the Archimedean point. And even at the risk of endangering the natural life process we expose the earth to universal, cosmic forces alien to nature's household. (Arendt 1958, p. 262)

Examples of the waste economy generated by the market's position as agonistic forum abound, but one is the increasing use of sports utility vehicles for personal transport. While it is unnecessary to focus on one commodity, the oxymoron 'sports utility' is such a spectacular moniker as to be emblematic of the problem. Despite their relatively high impact on the environment, despite the increasing scarcity and cost of oil, indeed, despite the fact that wars are being fought over this resource, the demand for these awkward, dangerous and uneconomical vehicles is increasing. One explanation for this is that they are large and, for the purposes of display, a large vehicle can be considered superior; furthermore their "utility" panders to a constructed notion of the possibility of freedom (Flint 2004)[3]. Certainly, sports utility vehicles are generally marketed as products that offer control and mastery of the environment. The expansion of the ownership of such vehicles is a result of the fact that they make a statement about their owners that the owners find they cannot make anywhere else, such as in a truly public political forum. What is interesting about this form of consumption is that it is not rational; it is pure spectacle. The consumer does not engage in all other forms of the spectacle just to become a rational utility maximiser at the point of consumption; consumption is also spectacular.

What this example illustrates is the 'hyper-reality' of consumption. Rather than our consumption being oriented towards utility, it is oriented towards display. Whereas in the time of *homo faber* products were produced and consumed because they enabled us to live, work and play more efficiently and productively, in the time of *homo spectaculum* products are produced and consumed in order to express something about the producer or consumer. While there is no doubt that consumption has always been seen as an element of expression, in spectacular society consumption is seen as the default method of expression. As discussed in the previous chapter, this change can be witnessed in the change in advertising methods—from advertising which identifies the utility of a product to advertising which identifies the meaning of a product. The more we "buy in" to these meanings, the more we anchor our sense of identity to consumption.

Expressing our spectacular selves through consumption is leading to a spectacular increase in consumption, precisely because consumption promises a satisfaction it cannot deliver. Humanity has used more goods and services since 1950 than in the previous 40 000 years of human history, yet since 1950 the incidence of depression has increased tenfold; significantly, the highest increase in depression has taken place amongst the highest consuming cultures (Monbiot 2000b). This correlation may suggest that the inbuilt obsolescence of many consumer goods is a possible cause of this statistic, but it is also the case that the society of *homo spectaculum* generates desire in such a way that no product is ever likely to satisfy the consumer in the way that it is purported to do so at purchase[4]. As an element of expression, a consumable good is impoverished—unlike personal expression, consumer goods lack uniqueness, relatedness and, generally, adaptability. Not only are newer and better products conjured by the market at a startling rate, but the meaning of each product is as transient as its marketing campaign. The fashion industry is the best example of this. As fashion changes, what one was wearing five years ago could not be worn this year as it no longer has the desired contemporary meaning. The dominant symptom of the society of *homo spectaculum* is that everything becomes fashion and, therefore, is redundant soon after it has been purchased. An obsession with objects has undermined the understanding that action is the source of happiness, hence the act of consuming itself becomes the source of happiness, and the obsolescence of commodities ensures that this activity must be engaged in continuously. The generation of the need for material goods as the only markers of public status is what has led to an unsustainable increase in the consumption of resources.

Homo Spectaculum and the International Order

The sharp spike in consumption driven by spectacular society has generated an extremely competitive demand for resources between nations. Oil is the prime commodity and, as a map of conflict throughout the world indicates, the presence of oil without the wealth to defend it tends to generate conflict. Even more catastrophic, though, is the jealous hoarding of wealth, technology and power by wealthy nations. At a time in human development which has been characterised as "post-scarcity", those sovereign nations with wealth are spending massive amounts of money to ensure no one else can gain access to it.

Despite some attempts by the United Nations to generate an international fraternity, no such engagement exists. Indeed, self-evident truths about all being equal are not even maintained to be true when national interest is at stake. It may be *reasonable* to identify that all people have equal rights, and use this as a foundation for understanding and agreement, but nationalism is an accomplished usurper of such communicative engagement. For this reason we can understand that the United States refuses to endorse an international criminal court, such as might have been used to bring Osama Bin Laden and Saddam Hussein to trial, on the basis that the United States does not wish to conform to the same rules as those they would use to judge others. It seems that the consciousness of *homo spectaculum* does not need to reconcile the deaths of the thousands of people who were killed in the process of enforced "regime change" with their otherwise inalienable right to life. Other nations are easily portrayed as competitors in order to ensure electoral and popular support; therefore, each must present the illusion to their citizens that their nation is stronger, wealthier and more successful than the others[5]. Nations, therefore, engage in the society of *homo spectaculum*, with the tangible result that the wealthier a nation becomes the more it spends on the defence of that wealth. As a corollary, the more obsessed with its own "private" affairs a nation becomes, the less it seeks to encounter and engage with other nations in some kind of public forum.

There may be progressive potential in this process of globalisation/centralisation. *Homo spectaculum* is aware of national boundaries but does not feel confined or defined by them. This characteristic distinguishes *homo spectaculum* from *homo faber*. While *homo faber* remains tied to the productive apparatus, the consumptive imperatives of *homo spectaculum* encourage exploration. As Habermas suggests in *The Structural Transformation of the Public*

Sphere, such population movement can be seen as conducive to the development of critical dialogues that lead to the development of a vibrant public sphere. Certainly, it is possible to argue that this change is leading to greater intersubjectivity on the part of *homo spectaculum* and that this, in turn, is responsible for the political ascendancy of international non-governmental organisations, such as Medecins Sans Frontiers and Amnesty International, which specifically try to address human issues without regard to political boundaries.

The political consciousness of *homo spectaculum,* however, remains restrained by its material limitations. Non-governmental organisations are serving as publics in lieu of a meaningful international public forum. While they are well intentioned, such organisations lack the legitimacy that comes from public office and are treated arbitrarily by institutions such as nation-states. While the society of *homo spectaculum* is increasingly responsive to global events, writers such as Clifford Bob note that this responsiveness is tailored by the spectacular imperatives of non-governmental organisations, rather than the demands of those requiring assistance; it is those who know how to stage a media event who receive the funding, rather than those who have the most reasonable claim upon it (Bob 2002). Without a discursive international political forum, the international political expression of *homo spectaculum* remains clumsy and uncritical.

The society of *homo spectaculum,* although it differs somewhat from that of *homo faber,* shares the common failing to foster critical thought and, therefore, is subject to similar problems. The society of *homo spectaculum* has catered to the public need for participation and interaction with public power by allowing this interaction to take place within the market; but the market itself does not promote the processes of thought and reason in the manner agonistic and deliberative democrats assure us is vital to the integrity of the public sphere. Subsequently our reality, humanity and identity are all casualties of the politics of the spectacle.

The Loss of the Public and the Absence of Democratic Inspiration

The rise of the society of *homo spectaculum* can be seen as an extension of the uncritical social realm because it removes the burden of showing reality from the immanent public and places a preconceived and uncritical social reality in its place. The opportunities for submersion in the unreal, or the virtually real, have exploded in the last thirty years (Pitkin 1998, p. 273). The internet and the associated "virtual realities" of *homo spectaculum* have allowed people to become ever more isolated and insulated in their virtual worlds; while these virtual worlds have, at the same time, become more responsive and tangible. This lack of public reality spells the demise of reason and the ascent of desire.

If we believe that the majority of the population have no pressing reason to be engaged with "reality" as such, then we may question whether it is necessary to advocate a democratic system of government at all. Without being preoccupied with consistency of reality and identity, it is possible to engage agonism in ever more spectacular and profitable ways. As has been mentioned, this is exactly what the market currently does.

The inability of contemporary representative political systems to engage with contemporary sovereignty has led to significant problems for humanity. The harmony between capitalism and liberalism is predicated upon the primacy of the individual as a basic, irreducible and impermeable unit. This assumption distinguishes the liberal model from the agonistic and deliberative models of democratic function. The latter two are predicated on the idea that individuals are inseparable from the world in which they come into being. The liberal model, instead, is predicated on the notion that individuals exist prior to, and in some way separately from, the world in which they act. This understanding of individuality makes sense of the world-alienation generated by modernity, and the formation of one's world independent of the public is the perfect motivation for continued capitalist expansion. The notion of world-alienation also underlies the liberal conception of the primary purpose of the state—namely, to ensure that one's liberty is not impinged upon by others. This conception of self, as somehow separate from the world or, indeed, in need of its own world, can be viewed to generate basic antagonism in light of the fact that we are still bound to the human condition of sharing one planet.

The Material Constraints of *Homo Spectaculum*

The impact of *homo faber* and *homo spectaculum* upon the environment suggests that reality itself may eventually become a constraint on the age of the spectacle. The loss of potable drinking water, arable land and pollutant-free food are all pressing and immediate concerns for a large proportion of the global population. These very real concerns generate their own communicative power as the experience of environmental degradation becomes more ubiquitous. Indeed, environmental disaster may be the first "general interest to which public opinion could refer to as a criterion" (Habermas 1989, p. 234) that generates the intersubjectivity necessary for ideal communication. The rising water levels are seen everywhere as real; throughout the human plurality of the biosphere such universal environmental changes may finally usher in some degree of intersubjectivity. The issue of environmental degradation thus forms a perfect test case for the abilities and constraints of public debate in the society of the spectacle.

The major obstacle which public action about environmental issues faces is that *homo spectaculum* has forgotten the value of real public space. The political public sphere is based on utilitarian economics to the extent that it alienates public expression. The remaining privately owned public spaces are either regarded cynically as exploitative or lauded for being immersive and responsive in a way that political public space is not. The result is that *homo spectaculum* perceives its reality and its identity as inherently related to the private spaces it chooses to inhabit. Those who suggest that there is some kind of real, natural and universal world which has imperatives beyond these spaces are taken to be hopeless romantics; primitives, hippies and idealists.

Consider the attempt to develop the political will to confront the problem of climate change. The first issue is that there are few who care about what happens to the global public. Those with a strong control over steering media—money and power—are those who are best able to control their private public spaces. So in Australia, the warming trend has generally been met by more air conditioners and greater power consumption—a private solution to a public problem[6]. On the other hand you have the people who are displaced by rising sea levels—such as the people of Kiribati, which is predicted to be the first country entirely submerged under the sea—however, insofar as they have control of steering media, they may migrate to a place where they can reinvent a private solution to a public problem.

If they do not have access to money or power, the desperate people of Kiribati are likely to try and invoke a public responsibility for ceasing the effects of global warming, and it's likely they will employ the tools of ideal speech in order to do so. They will attempt to be included in conversations about global warming and when they do, they will discuss their problems according to what they feel are understandable and universal interests, in order to use the force of reason to influence the outcome. Unfortunately, as they do not have access to money or power, it is unlikely that they will be able to get much attention from the otherwise spectacularly engaged global public. Certainly, using the internet, the poor of Kiribati could warn people of their cause, making use of the rhizomatic elements of the internet to call for help. However, creating a web page does not mean that page will be viewed. And considering the commercial imperatives of mass media organisations, it's unlikely that a news editor would choose to run this story unless the story becomes spectacular, possibly at the moment where Kiribati finally disappears under the waves altogether.

The news editors, as with the news editors' readers and viewers, live in the society of the spectacle. The editors and their readers spend their day moving between private spaces—these spaces are entertaining, immersive and responsive—and they preclude the need to engage with the real world. In fact throughout the day the editors are more likely to repeatedly encounter celebrity gossip than they are to encounter the idea that we share one common world for which we all must assume responsibility. As such, when the editors make a choice about what news to include in the night's bulletin, they know that celebrity news will have real resonance and meaning with their audience, while news of a few poor people struggling to live on an island somewhere has very little relevance—and thus the issue of the public effect of global warming is ignored for the night.

On the other hand, the spectacular citizen who could choose to spend their evening searching the internet for a more real and pervasive understanding of the world, is unlikely to do so. The conditions of spectacular existence are quite exhausting, insofar as in every scenario there is a constant renegotiation of identity and meaning. During the day *homo spectaculum* is a dynamic worker, whose sense of identity and meaning is tied up in the work they do. When they take breaks they are sure to display themselves as fun and attentive friends and colleagues, as they know that such relationships are another source of meaning in life. On the way home, they may drop by a shopping centre, where they are confronted with the issue of what their purchases are saying about them. When they get home they are expected to become a master of epicurean delights and to respond, wherever possible, to the extended conversations taking place on their social networking sites. When *homo spectaculum* wishes to escape this endless changing of masks, they do not have the option of escaping to be their "real selves" in the "real world" as they can't say for sure these things exist. Instead of going online to find out what is "really" happening in the world, say to the people of Kiribati, they choose to go somewhere to escape for a while and engage in a useless pursuit—possibly an online game or watching a movie on their massive digital television. All the while they become more aware of the satisfaction they gain from their private world and less interested and acquainted with what happens in public.

Every three or four years, *homo spectaculum* gets the opportunity to engage in the public political process—they get a choice: vote for the candidate who insists that we should pay more to curb the effect of carbon emissions upon the environment, or vote for the candidate who is offering government money to stimulate the economy—just enough to buy a bigger television with the latest 3D capabilities. When there is no concept of the importance of the public and no understanding of what the public gives us, it is hard to imagine that citizens will seek to use politics for anything but private ends.

Terrorism, Economic Crisis and the Spectacle

The loss of engagement with reality and reality forming publics produces some tangible results when reality proves somewhat irrepressible. Terrorism and the economic cycles of boom and crisis are two highly evident aspects of the age of the spectacle. In both terrorism and economic crisis, one sees the catastrophic reconciliation of otherwise separate perceptions of reality. These incidences stand as the hallmarks of age of the spectacle because the reconciliations, syntheses or confrontations between these realities tend to, in themselves, be spectacular.

Economic Crisis

The boom/bust cycle of international financial markets is an inherent element of the detached systemic nature of those markets. While economists have uncovered multiple causes for global financial crises, each cause is linked to the abstraction of systemic rationality away from lifeworld legitimacy—or the development of economic systems to disregard reality. As an example of this paradigm of market failure, the 2008 Global Financial Crisis has been variously attributed to the growth of the housing bubble, easy credit conditions, sub-prime and predatory lending, deregulation, overleveraging of debt and the incorrect pricing of risk. A brief explanation of these mechanics indicates how abstraction was based upon abstraction to the point where the system could not legitimately reconcile itself with the lifeworld.

The story of the 2008 Global Financial Crisis began with an insistence that an abstraction could do a more useful job of modelling finance than reality. Confronted with the inefficient aspect of reality that people sometimes could not afford to pay their loans, and realising that this undermined confidence in the market and thus financial growth, bankers invented a system of spreading that risk amongst financial institutions so that the risk of lending "virtually" disappeared. As a result of the mitigated risk of lending, financial institutions made many more high risk loans and offered far more "flexible and responsive" products to encourage more lending. These products allowed borrowers to also take more risks with their money and, among other things, allowed more people to take out loans for houses. As a result of the greater demand for houses the prices of houses inflated, as did the loans needed to purchase them and the equity associated with them. Eventually, the amount of debt accumulated to the point where repayments became problematic and people began to default on their payments. Essentially their real wages hadn't kept up with the spectacular optimism of the lenders. The result was a sequential shattering of the abstractions which had taken place. As people couldn't afford their loans, banks began to foreclose and credit agencies started demanding payment. With many people losing their houses, the values of property declined significantly, leaving many people with loans greater than their property values and causing more foreclosures and even lower property values. Banks, as a result, found themselves in possession of a lot of debt for an ever growing amount of bad assets, and became increasingly cautious about extending credit. Because all financial institutions had taken part in the risk mitigation in the first place, the failure of the financial sector as a whole led to a chronic and further slowing of the economy[7]. Only extreme measures on behalf of governments, such as buying up bad assets, bailing out banks and providing stimulus spending to the economy (by increasing the national deficit or selling off public assets), managed to improve the confidence of commerce to the point where people once again began borrowing and spending.

One particularly interesting explanation for why concerns for reality, or a public interest, were disregarded at various stages of this process has come from *Financial Times* editor Gillian Tett, who attempted to describe the causes of the crisis from an anthropological perspective. The first thing that she points out is that the JP Morgan bankers who found a way to make debt "risk-free" had developed their own systemic expertise which distanced them from the legitimating principles of the rest of the world.

> Bankers...operate as a tightly defined group, with specific cultural patterns and a quasi language (or jargon) of their own. Also...bankers are generally trained to think in rigid 'silos' and, as a result, find it hard to see how their overall system operates, or to see the contradictions in their own rhetoric and internal organizations. (Tett 2009b, p. 6)

Ideally, the actions of these bankers may have also been scrutinised by journalists. However, as Tett points out, they were under no duress to speak publicly about their plans.

> Twentyfirst century journalism tends to assume that newspaper stories can only 'work' for readers or viewers if they feature stories about recognized, named individuals who can supply 'on the record' quotes, supplemented with verifiable facts and tangible events. Such elements can usually be found with stories about the stock market, where there are named individuals (company CEOs), events and facts (such as quoted prices). However, in the debt and derivatives world of 2004, bankers generally loathed publicity and would rarely give 'on the record' quotes. Moreover, it was difficult to get price or trading data since deals were typically made in private, not on public exchanges, and discrete events seemed few and far between. (Tett 2009b, p. 6)

These bankers moved within a series of private worlds, never having to rationalise what they were doing in public. The government regulation of the industry, which may have halted the implementation of the debt mitigation scheme on the basis of the public interest, had been largely done away with. As Tett explains:

> To a certain extent that was because many policymakers adhered to an intellectual framework that assumed that finance would be most efficient without government interference, and that innovation and free market forces were always good. (Tett 2009b, p. 7)

Finally, where the media were apparently aware of the problem with debt mitigation and the resulting overheating of the economy, they were unwilling to bring this to the public's attention until the problem became spectacular enough to warrant their attention.

> Another key factor was the social silence and the fact that although credit markets were overheating, they did not meet the usual definition of a journalistic "story," since the subject matter seemed too complex, technical and dull, dressed up in a jargon that only bankers appeared able to understand. Thus there was little public debate about the frenetic activity, and precious little pressure on policymakers to challenge the received wisdom about how credit markets were supposed to work. (Tett 2009b, p. 7)

Seen in this light, economic crisis seems to be an inherent part of the society of the spectacle. As with the other spectacular failure of the market in the 1930s, the response to the crisis on behalf of the government of *homo faber* was to do whatever it takes, borrow and spend whatever was necessary, in order to get people consuming again and get the financial system back on its feet. But for a few moments in every such crisis the failure of such systems to adequately encounter reality is laid bare; the aim of representative democratic government is systemic integrity, not the integrity of the lifeworld.

Terrorism

The corruption of the international economy for the benefit of the wealthiest portion of that economy is a clear example of systemic legitimacy becoming abstracted away from a general, universalisable interest. The level of systemic abstraction reached by *homo spectaculum* is probably the most understandable explanation for terrorism as a concept and terrorism as a movement, as those who seek to employ terrorist acts are those who are otherwise excluded from participating in negotiating the legitimacy of the systems which determine their lifeworld. This is a complicated way of explaining terrorism as a product of political, economic and social exclusion of ideologies which are irreconcilable with spectacular society. The representative democratic system, oriented to the values of *homo faber*, views terrorism as the irrational act of a dangerous "other". According to the utilitarian ends of *homo faber*, those who insist on trying to maintain a public legitimacy based upon ideology or myths can only be an impediment to the smooth functioning of society.

The most concerning aspect of the designation of those outside the system as terrorists or potential terrorists is that it stifles public discussion. According to agonistic and deliberative principles the only way to reasonably deal with difference is to encounter it and in the process seek to achieve an understanding acceptable to both parties. *Homo spectaculum's* capacity to understand difference far exceeds that of *homo faber* and *animal laborans*. There are, however, structural impediments which tend to prevent this understanding taking place. As mentioned above, the political realm of *homo faber* cannot see the value of ideologues beyond their productive capacity and thus seeks to largely exclude these dysfunctional others. Anyone outside or against the society of spectacles is designated terrorist. Meanwhile the private public realms of *homo spectaculum* only examine terrorists at the points where they make enough of a spectacle of themselves to warrant attention.

A brief consideration of news values highlights why *homo spectaculum* is unlikely to be exposed to the reality of the remainder of the human population—what is in fact the majority world[8]. News values are the principles which determine whether a story is "newsworthy" and they include impact, proximity, prominence, human interest, novelty, conflict and currency. The more any story possesses these values, the more likely the story is to be told. It is clear that unless the majority world shares our public sphere, then it is unlikely to be thought of as proximate or prominent. Indeed as the lives of *homo spectaculum* become ever more abstracted away from the realities of the majority world, the possibility of sharing a similar understanding of human interest, currency or impact also declines. This leaves us with novelty and conflict; so it should not be surprising that it is stories of novelty and conflict—particularly in the case of a threat to the spectacular world—that tend to dominate our images of that world.

> So far as the United States seems to be concerned, it is only a slight overstatement to say that Moslems and Arabs are essentially seen as either oil suppliers or potential terrorists. Very little of the detail, the human density, the passion of Arab-Moslem life has entered the awareness of even those people whose profession it is to report the Arab world. What we have instead is a series of crude, essentialized caricatures of the Islamic world presented in such a way as to make that world vulnerable to military aggression. (Said 1980)

Of course, the failure to engage with the majority world causes an ever greater schism between the society of the spectacle and the rest of the world. The result of this is a growing incommensurability between these two worlds which at times seems akin to speciation[9]. Put simply, *homo spectaculum* is so far removed from the issues of wide scale violence, repression and desperation that these issues prove hard to relate to. For example, when one of the most violent genocides in history took place in Rwanda, with 800,000 people murdered in less than a year, the top news story in the US was the murder of Nicole Brown Simpson–OJ Simpson's wife ("Wire services pick top stories of 1994" 1995). In fact, a USA Today poll of the "Top 25 Biggest News Stories" over the 25 years leading up to 2007, rated the Rwandan genocide as the 19th biggest news story, behind the Challenger space shuttle explosion (17th), the death of 80 Branch Davidians (16th), the police beating of Rodney King (15th), the death of Princess Diana (12th), the Monica Lewinsky scandal (7th) and the Simpson murder at number 5 (Hampson 2007). This list relates the sense of detachment felt towards those "beyond the pale" of spectacular society; a detachment that means the death of a famous wealthy person deserves more attention than the deaths of hundreds of thousands of unspectacular people.

Terrorism and economic crisis present two spectacular manifestations of the politics of the spectacle. In both cases, crises are bought about as a result of the absence of a political public sphere which is inclusive and allows claims to truth to be redeemed. Without an opportunity to provide a consensual check or counterbalance to systemic realms of communication such systems are free to abstract themselves away from the general and universalisable principles which would otherwise constitute the lifeworld. As the systemic domains of legitimacy become more spectacularly abstracted from the realities of our material existence, the real limitations of the world are ignored until the tension between the spectacular and the real becomes too great and the spectacular momentarily shatters. During times of economic crisis and terrorist acts, when the media and professional organisations are screaming apocalypse, it can seem confronting how normal the world beyond the screens continues to be. These moments of encountering reality remind us that these crises are systemic crises, not crises of the lifeworld and they should serve to remind us that the lifeworld should regulate the system, not the other way around. Of course, at these points of crisis, the political system established by *homo faber* remains in spectacular society to use the machinery of the state to ensure the resumption of production and consumption, and so systemic dominance resumes.

Two Visions of the Future

I shall now examine two possible futures that are suggested through this understanding of the manifestations of the society of the spectacle. These futures are constructed according to what we should expect to see resulting from the dominance of *homo spectaculum* in light of deliberative and agonistic theories. The difference in the two visions is based upon the centrality of our earthly, natural reality as an element of our shared lifeworld. In the first instance, the growing illegitimacy of the society of *homo spectaculum* may well lead to a conflict in those societies in which lifeworld legitimacy is still a precondition for the use of power. In the second instance, the development of *homo spectaculum* beyond the legitimacy restrained by the real, natural world suggests the possibility of moving beyond the natural and escaping the bounds of the earth.

The Rise of the International Proletariat

I have previously presented the argument that those who control capital have sought to appropriate public space in order to continually stimulate production. I have also argued that, in the process, there has been a change in the nature of the means of production and a change in the relationship between self and world. As such I have borrowed from the Marxist view that capital is the driving force of contemporary political change, and it is interesting at this point to scrutinise the validity of Marx's predictions. Marx predicted that capital would continue to expand and conquer new territory until it could expand no further, at which point it would invent and reorganise points within its territory in order to simulate this expansion[10]. Marx also predicted the development of the world market and a communications network that would undermine the constraints of space and time in order to stimulate growth (Marx 1973a, pp. 408–539). All these things will conspire, Marx argues, to develop the tools and consciousness of a revolutionary proletariat (Marx 1973b, p. 73). It remains eminently possible that this consciousness is developing in the global working class and may conflict with the consciousness of *homo spectaculum* in such a way as to generate progress.

While production is increasingly removed from the capital intensive workplace of *homo spectaculum*, this does not mean that the alienation generated though production simply vanishes. Instead, the globalisation of the market can be understood to have merely enabled the outsourcing of the alienation of production.

> The bourgeoisie, by the rapid improvement of all instruments of production, by immensely facilitated means of communication, draws all, even the most barbarian, nations into civilisation...It compels all nations, on pain of extinction, to adopt the bourgeois mode of production; it compels them to introduce what it calls civilisation into their midst, i.e., to become bourgeois themselves. In one word, it creates a world after its own image. (Marx 1973b, p. 71)

For Marx, the globalisation of the market and the subsequent globalisation of communication is the precondition for a worldwide revolutionary consciousness. The spectacular imperatives of *homo spectaculum* still require the productive efforts of *homo faber*, and while maintaining the machines may be alienating, the production of the spectacle still depends upon such machines. The need to resolve this tension implies that the emergence of *homo spectaculum* may yet generate progress in a Marxist sense.

As many have pointed out previously, the system of international trade operates under extremely detached systems of legitimacy that are based on claims to truth that are not easily redeemed[11]. While *homo spectaculum* demands a more spectacular degree of consumption, the spectacular society requires the developing world to replicate the politics of *homo faber*. The view that those in the majority world accept this role because they so desperately want to be part of world trade relies upon the assumption that they will adopt the material fixations of *homo faber*. In order to generate those fixations, the material society of *homo spectaculum* is presented to the rest of the world as innately virtuous and good. Yet the demands exacted upon the world by *homo spectaculum* are actually irreconcilable with what the real world can produce. As a global community we are currently consuming more natural resources than the planet can sustain (Global Footprint Network 2010) and *homo spectaculum* is responsible for the vast majority of that consumption. Therefore the suggestion that we might all become spectacular is not actually reconcilable with the reality of what the earth can provide.

Nevertheless, the desirability of spectacular existence is only ever presented on a screen; it is rarely deeply examined. *Homo spectaculum* markets itself through the productive capacities of the military-industrial-media-entertainment complex[12]. At the same time *homo spectaculum* isolates its workers by denying them access to anything other than an instrumental public realm; for nothing other than a representative liberal democracy is permitted to be seen as legitimate despite *homo spectaculum's* own alienation from such a public. Such a public realm ensures productivity but the imposition of a public realm that is essentially alienating may also precipitate a revolutionary consciousness.

As Arendt predicted, the failure to create a public realm that reconciles humanity with reality either precipitates a disregard for reality or the creation of a new public realm in opposition. Amid all these situations of unequal relations it remains the case that the majority of the world's *animal laborans* are excluded from the decision making forums that affect their lives. Along with the fact that working conditions are defined by repressive national governments—which attract investment by banning workers from political organisation—international political institutions, such as the United Nations, fail to provide or demand legitimate democratic accountability[13]. While the internet presents the possibility for increasing communicative action on an international level, the current nature of international institutions reflects the values of *homo faber*. The three major commitments of the United Nations Economic and Social Development Forum are to eradicate poverty, address underemployment and promote social integration. This forum avoids communicatively engaging with the meaning of development, and these three commitments are striking, insofar as they address the purely functional concerns of *homo faber*—have money, have a job, be functional. Becoming global remains a process of assimilation rather than integration because the international public sphere is dominated by the values of *homo faber*.

In such a situation *animal laborans* is deprived of a correct outlet for action and may respond through an imaginary vengeance, whereby their interests are identified in a fundamental rejection of reason. Subsequently,

> where the institutions and discourses are missing that could permit that potential antagonisms manifest themselves under an agonistic mode, the danger exists that instead of a struggle among adversaries, what will take place is a war between enemies. (Mouffe 2000a, pp. 30-31)

The inability of vast quantities of the world's people to gain access to a meaningful political forum results in the transformation of agonism into antagonism (as people fail to recognise what they share in common). This phenomenon, when viewed in light of the theories of Arendt and Habermas, can be seen as a direct and simple result of the absence of public space that can translate antagonism into agonism. As Arendt suggests, the failure of a public realm tends to generate the construction of new public realms. The real, natural constraints upon the age of the spectacle suggest that the international proletariat may eventually overcome the society of the spectacle, either through evolution or revolution.

The Rise of the Cyborg

The final question which remains is whether *homo spectaculum* needs to be reconciled with our earthly reality at all. Donna Haraway has suggested that this reconciliation with reality is barely possible, that there is no point referring to a natural order which is always an abstraction (Haraway 1991). Jean-Francois Lyotard has gone further and hinted that our detachment from the world is, in some sense, the foundation of our escape from its limitations (Lyotard 1992). Arendt's theory is fundamentally opposed to world alienation yet if we distil Arendt's pronouncements about founding we can interpret the benefits of the escape from the world from an essentially phenomenological perspective; that is, we can believe that such a loss provides us with a new opportunity to rediscover our humanity as independent of the world. Certainly, Habermas's theories leave open the possibility that we might actually evolve away from, or beyond, the earth, as communicative action's emphasis on consensual legitimacy provides us with the ability to achieve emancipation without recourse to the "real".

Following the loss of a public forum in which to understand the real, and the subsequent emergence of control as control of the self, there is much to suggest that the world has also lost the means to chart a course back to "reality".

> By the late twentieth century, our time, a mythic time, we are all chimeras, theorized and fabricated hybrids of machine and organism; in short, we are cyborgs. The cyborg is our ontology; it gives us our politics. The cyborg is a condensed image of both imagination and material reality, the two joined centres structuring any possibility of historical transformation. (Haraway 1991, p. 150)

Haraway uses the cyborg as a metaphor, as a way of moving beyond the nature/culture dichotomy and, importantly, to explore 'how we [might] craft more ethical, liveable lives for all human and non-human organisms' (Grebowicz & Merrick 2011). Thus, even as she escapes an *a priori* assumption about the natural conditions of life, she re-establishes the need for us to live, relate and make meaning in an ethical way. As discussed in Chapter Seven, the partial, hybrid and fragmented subjectivity of *homo spectaculum* has a number of attributes which invoke "the possibility of connectedness and survival beyond innocence in an impure world" (Sofoulis 2002, p. 57).

A more extreme interpretation of the culture/nature relationship has been suggested by the extropian movement. Based upon the principles of perpetual progress, self-transformation, practical optimism, intelligent technology, open society, self-direction and rational thinking, the aim of extropianism is specifically to overcome the natural limitations of an earth-bound humanity (More 1998). Whereas Haraway uses the cyborg as a metaphor to think about how we relate to the world under spectacular conditions, the extropian movement argues that we can pursue a transhuman future by moving beyond the constraints of nature. For the extropians, imaginative self-directed experimentation is the key to this transhuman evolution.

When related to this perspective, a commonly held reality can be restricting, denying people the opportunities to indulge private desires which develop their own energies and their own potentials. If there is no need to reconcile our desires with the constrictions implied by our shared natural existence then the reconciliation of all reason to a conception of public good has no innate force of compulsion. Hence it is possible to envisage a future in which there is no politics as such, just an incredibly deliberative and reflexive market that caters to isolated individuals in their screened environments. Such a future would promote the development of desire-satisfaction as opposed to reason-satisfaction—becoming more responsive, immersive and gratifying. This future would alter the human condition to such an extent that the "human" traits of thought, speech and action may no longer be a suitable basis for political systems.

The reconceptualisation of the political following the concurrent developments of information and communication technologies and postmodern philosophy has tended to avoid engaging with the human search for the truth and moved towards imagining what might come from abandoning such a search, or reinventing that search with the aid of unlimited imagination. Relative to the restrictions and violence of the public realm of *homo faber*, *homo spectaculum* rejoices in such freedom, and humanity may require this energy to move beyond the earth. It is not, however, the role of this book to imagine what the ideal form of life is, rather, it has been to discuss the ideal form of public communication. If communication is not public, if there is no compulsion to reconcile our private lives with what is real, or shared, then politics can be understood to be a truly private matter.

This discussion has been conducted in order to illustrate the possible futures that await *homo spectaculum* according to the theories espoused in this book. There are optimistic possibilities; however, if we are going to pursue the extropian project or attempt to coordinate our survival as humans, the course of future action is likely to require communicative action coordination on the largest scale. In a more pessimistic sense, the conflict between systemic and lifeworld realities may be unsustainable and may well result in the spectacular decline of *homo spectaculum*. I would suggest we should not demand that other people submit to the spectacle, as it is the attempt to do so that is causing friction between the society of the spectacle and the remainder of the world. Liberal democratic societies have traditionally been lauded because they avoid conflict by forcing agonism from the political arena into the market. However, their reliance on a continual increase in production means that reconciliation between *homo spectaculum* and worldly reality now tends to lead to conflict. The historic alternative to open, understanding inclusion is for *homo spectaculum* to fight and subjugate those who refuse the spectacle. This is not a way to resolve conflict, but to generate it. Under these conditions, liberalism as a peaceful element of democracy loses its normative appeal, as does democracy itself.

CHAPTER SEVEN

Constructing a Critical Democratic Theory

Shell smashed, juices flowing
wings twitch, legs are going,
don't get sentimental,
it always ends up drivel.
One day, I am gonna grow wings

—Radiohead 'Let Down' (1997)

Of course it is possible for humanity to avoid its spectacular democratic failure. This chapter suggests what can be done to reinvigorate democratic practices. By its very nature, critical theory must be a theory of change. While the theories discussed so far portray what has gone wrong with late industrial democracies, what I am interested in is how we can use these understandings to reinstate personal political action as a hallmark of democratic societies. One of the central aims of this book is to present an elaboration of the ways in which it is possible to read agonistic and deliberative theories as complementary when thinking about how democracy might be redesigned. While I have suggested that synthesising Habermas's and Arendt's theories presents a pessimistic picture for democracy, I believe it is also possible to identify the potential of constructing a new form of spectacular politics. In this chapter I shall briefly summarise how deliberative and agonistic theories can be understood to be positive about the democratic potentials of *homo spectaculum*. The deliberative view that communication is the basis of social progress and the agonistic understanding of the benefits of plural interpretations of reality lead us to the conclusion that while *homo spectaculum* may not be encouraged to engage in ideal democratic practices, there are elements of spectacular existence that have the potential to promote and enable a critical public engagement. Indeed there are elements of spectacular subjectivity which present *homo spectaculum* as an ideal democratic actor.

The impact of digital technology—notably the internet—upon the public sphere also produces some positive potential for both agonistic and deliberative democracy. Digital technology dramatically extends the opportunity for deliberation; and at the same time, through extending this possibility for engagement, the same technology enables this engagement to be ever more expressive. In short, the rise of the internet allows for communication which is simultaneously more engaging and more critical than that offered by the mass-mediated public sphere.

Habermas and Arendt as Complementary Theorists

As discussed in the introduction, the basic area of agreement between Habermas and Arendt is in their shared understanding of the communicative composition of power. This shared understanding is reflected in Arendt's statements concerning the meaning of public life deriving from the plural engagement with (and composition of) reality (Arendt 1958, p. 57) and Habermas's insistence that fundamental normative agreement must form the basis of action coordination as an antidote to the influence of steering media. As a result of this understanding of the composition of power, I have pointed out how each theorist seeks to integrate personal agency with public power.

Given the communicative constitution of power, both Habermas and Arendt seek to ground this power in the most fundamentally justifiable ways possible. Habermas, therefore, understands legitimate power as constituted by the shared assumptions and beliefs that unite the members of a lifeworld. Similarly, the legitimate power of Arendt's public debate is constituted by an ability to appeal to the shared assumptions and beliefs of the given public. She contends that this purpose is expressly served by narratives—or the telling of stories. Arendt suggests that one way of understanding a public and the people in it is to listen to the stories they tell amongst themselves. The more commonly acceptable the story, the more it is told, the more legitimacy it has. Here, Arendt echoes narrative theorist Hayden White's view that narratives have the ability to transcend difference by identifying commonality. Thus,

> far from being one code among many that a culture may utilize for endowing experience with meaning, narrative is a meta-code, a human universal on the basis of which transcultural messages about the nature of a shared reality can be transmitted. (White 1987, p. 1)

Whilst there are important differences in the aesthetic qualities of communicative action as constituting the lifeworld and narrative as bearing the legitimacy of a shared public understanding, in both views the bounds of legitimacy are taken to be constituted by commonly identifiable and communicable norms (Benhabib 2002, p. 357). While narrative devices, such as rhetoric, can be employed strategically in order to compel or instruct, the reflexive and discursive character of narrative implies that its primary orientation is to be understood. Similarly, the discursive element of Habermas's ideal communication seems to suggest that the telling of stories is a good way to move towards understanding. Therefore narratives provide an avenue to express the "context-transcending validity claims" (Habermas 1996, p. 4) that can form the basis of agreement. Insofar as they transcend contexts and defy mechanical replication, narratives provide a dramatic improvement on knowledge as a basis for social organisation.

Both Habermas and Arendt emphasise the importance of harnessing the critical potential of public speech and believe that the place of this speech is important. The divergence in their theories lies in the way they believe that this critical function operates. For Habermas, the public forum generates critical discourse by scrutinising the way stories are told. For Arendt, the public forum generates critical discourse by providing a space for personal stories to be reconciled with what is real. This serves a critical function not only by allowing critical "deliberative" discourse, but also because public engagement fulfils a private need for "agonistic" disclosure. Thus Arendt's public sphere serves not only in a deliberative capacity but also in an aesthetic sense, by allowing a space for expression. Habermas sees the communicative ideal as inspiring a critical public; Arendt understands that a critical public inspires thought.

Whereas other theorists have sought to distinguish Arendt's and Habermas's projects, at this point I would instead like to emphasise how their ideas about expressive critical conduct actually complement each other. For instance, for those who suggest that Habermas's deliberative democracy presents a hegemonic version of discourse that carries a necessary political violence of exclusion[1], Arendt's notion of the inescapably plural nature of the public forum suggests that such hegemony is something of a practical impossibility. It becomes clear that Arendt and Habermas share this understanding when one realises that Habermas's requirement that claims to truth be discursively redeemed is intended to draw out and celebrate this irrepressible plurality, as opposed to exclude it[2]. On the other hand, Arendt's agonistic democracy has been criticised for relying on a competitive expression of uniqueness that too easily "results in universal suspicion and resentment" (O'Sullivan 2000). In this instance Habermas's conditions of ideal communication provide a reflexive mode of communication that can ensure that agonism does not develop into antagonism.

The similarity between Habermas's and Arendt's ideas here is based upon other shared preconceptions. Namely, both Arendt and Habermas believe that there is an intersubjectivity that is achievable between all human subjects; or rather, that there is something about being human which endows us with the inalienable ability to make meaning together. Arendt contends that there is a human *need* to make meaning together, which gives rise to the construction of the public realm (Arendt 1958, p. 180). Habermas, in turn, argues that the act of understanding presupposes the ability to meaningfully share and engage with each other. In the process of public dialogue the critical faculties of communication and thought are stimulated, validating the self and the public realm in the process. Once again, the themes of self-validation and critical action can be developed concurrently through the intersection of Arendt's description of thought and Habermas's idealisation of communication. In each case the idea is to anchor decision making to the most critical, reflective and legitimate procedures.

Arendt's and Habermas's democratic theories are also largely complementary insofar as they both present the possibility of human emancipation as something which is already immanent to the individual. What I hope to have derived from reading Habermas and Arendt in this way is that we understand that emancipative acts—asking that claims to truth be discursively redeemed, and distinguishing oneself through public challenge and argument— are actually accessible to all of us, even *homo spectaculum*. Indeed, as shall be explored forthwith, *homo spectaculum* may well have a greater propensity for redemption and distinction than either *animal laborans* or *homo faber*.

It is not my intention to suggest that deliberative and agonistic democratic theories are the same or interchangeable, but rather to identify how they complement each other in terms of increasing our understanding of the critical deficit of liberal democracies. This process of identification unearthed a common understanding of the social nature of individuality, which stands in contrast to the liberal conception of the individual existing prior to and, in many senses, above the society in which that individual is formed. By alerting us to the communicative composition of power and highlighting the importance of democratic interaction in making sure that individual sovereignty is both critical and engaged with the world, Arendt and Habermas present a common front against the abuses of liberal democracy. Both oppose a conception of individuals as existing outside of the communicative community of which they are part. This understanding of the central relation between communicative spaces and the subjectivity of the individual suggests that deliberative and agonistic theories are more suitable for democracy within the digital public sphere, where traditional communication models of information passing from sender to receiver have been turned on their head.

While liberal democracy is based upon the existence of individual rights prior to the individual's engagement with the world, Habermas and Arendt both emphasise the symbiotic connection between the self (and its rights) and the world. Through their understanding of the communicative composition of power both theorists emphasise the identity forming aspects of the interaction between self and world. They therefore design their emancipatory projects around ensuring a critical interaction between self and world—notably involving thought and consideration—rather than a passive reception of self and world. They each identify chimerical moments in history in which the interaction between self and world was both critical and engaging as those moments where we witnessed truly democratic politics. They also identify the ways in which the critical and engaging elements of political forums have been usurped and replaced by more passive modes of reality reception.

Habermas and Arendt identify that world reception and world creation are integrally related to the constitution of the self. They both emphasise the point that engagement and control of the self translates directly to engagement and control of the world. What they conspire against is the passive construction of self in relation to a world that is determined by the constructions of those who control the identity forming contexts of public space. This is the threat carried by the public space of *homo faber*—which is instrumental and valued only in terms of its ends; and the "private" public spaces of *homo spectaculum*—which are gratifying but also transient, rhetorical and irrational. Habermas and Arendt believe that it is possible to reassert the importance of self in world creation through democratic action, action that resists the passive reception of reality and engages in the construction of the world. It is in this context that they present their democratic theories as emancipative theories, taking the view that it is through aspiring toward a sound democratic form that a freer and better human existence can be generated.

Applying Agonistic and Deliberative Theories to Contemporary Conditions

There are certain elements of the age of the spectacle which raise the possibility of agonistic actors creating a spectacle of themselves by engaging in critical public debates; however, these same elements have blurred the definition of what exactly is public. Dana Villa has described this dilemma:

> From an Arendtian perspective, the challenge of a 'postmodern' politics is to maintain the link between action and publicity in a context where the institutionalised public sphere is deeply compromised and the definition of what is properly 'public' is perhaps the most hotly contested issue of all. (Villa 1997, p. 201)

The argument developed here is that the fragmentation of publics, realities and identities that occurs following the colonisation of the lifeworld fundamentally undermines the link between action and publicity and does not facilitate their reconciliation with reality. The effect this has on the emancipatory potential of democratic action undermines the very basis of Arendt's hope for the consistent emancipatory force of natality. Whilst Habermas's theory is much more conducive to generating legitimacy even in the conditions of a highly "abstracted" lifeworld, it is arguable that the loss of a real public undermines the individual's concerns for legitimacy, reality and care for the "other".

Habermas acknowledges that the development of a completely cynical consciousness undermines the emancipatory potential of democratic processes. The condition of detachment from political power, which I have suggested characterises *homo spectaculum*, is such that it undermines Habermas's own theory that actors seeking legitimacy are the guardians of democratic deliberation. Following the alienation of politics

> law has to be transformed into an instrument of behaviour control; and democratic majority decision turns into an inconsequential spectacle of deception and self deception. A capitulation of constitutional principles in the face of overwhelming social complexity cannot be ruled out. Should this occur, our concepts of justice and democracy will change, and citizens' normative self-understanding, which still exists in our latitudes today, will undergo a radical transformation. (Habermas 2002, p. 242)

The emancipative potential of communicative action relies upon the existence of actors who are not thoroughly cynical and disillusioned with the processes of politics and law but who, rather, share concepts of democracy and justice that are in some sense inherent to a citizen's normative understanding of self. I assert that *homo spectaculum is* rightly cynical and disillusioned in regard to politics and, thus, if there is any hope for democratic emancipation, it lies in an irrepressibly *human* search for reality and identity.

Hannah Arendt's suggestion that agonism is linked to an instinctual human desire to display suggests that world creation *is* a fundamental human imperative. It is her argument for the persistence of agonism that offers most hope that democracy might be revived. Although the political life may never be the domain of the many, in her work, along with John Stuart Mill and Frederick Nietzsche, she insists that there is an innate human potential for emancipation. Our search for truth, individually or as a society, binds us to an agreement to engage critically with the world during moments of founding. Marcuse also describes this innate search for truth as a fundamentally emancipatory force.

> Inasmuch as the struggle for truth 'saves' reality from destruction, truth commits and engages human existence. It is the essentially human project. If man has learned to see and know what really is, he will act in accordance with truth. Epistemology is in itself ethics, and ethics is epistemology. (Marcuse 1964, p. 125)

The search for truth is a process of the elimination of the untenable elements of rhetoric and an attempt to come to an understanding of what is real. If *homo spectaculum* retains its natural human inclination towards seeking reality and identity, then there are many reasons to be optimistic about the politics of the spectacle.

Hence, in this book I am seeking to assert the centrality of Arendt's position on the importance of "natural right" to democratic emancipation[3]. On the one hand, I believe that Arendt, who locates the need for democratic expression within the faculties of thought, speech, action and the creation of new life, thereby identifies one fundamental imperative for reasonable action coordination—to care for the world that sustains us. At the same time the idea that human action is the only possible source of emancipation and that our humanity is somehow irrepressible, implies that the power to be emancipated lies in our own hands and *is not* constrained by socially determined subjectivities such as *homo spectaculum*. This is an important idea given the ascent of information and communication technologies—and it is a way to read Arendt as positive about the democratic potential of cyberspace.

Arendt's argument is located in her view as to what it is to be human, and the rights granted to us by our human abilities. The prospect of finite abilities is not a problem for Arendt, who believes that such abilities may yet become immortalised in the public realm and achieve a degree of permanence. Finiteness haunts *homo spectaculum*, however, who has lost such a realm. Any critical democratic theory should seek to resolve the tension between a virtual reality, defined by Habermas as composed of a series of fragmented and independently legitimated subsystems, and the conditions of real human existence. Arendt's theories constitute a source of optimism concerning *homo spectaculum's* moments of founding in the information age, but only if we accept that *homo spectaculum* has certain human elements—a need for identity, reality and natality—that are, in some sense, inalienable. If we accept this then the communicative potential of virtual reality provides a basis for optimism about the development of internet technology.

A Positive Synthesis: *Homo Spectaculum* in a World of Petite Narratives[4]

In many ways, the positive democratic potentials of *homo spectaculum* arise from *homo spectaculum's* ability to engage with reality as a series of small narratives. Due to the unresponsiveness of the dominant narratives of *homo faber*, *homo spectaculum* is increasingly likely to draw upon more interesting, exotic, marginalised and subaltern narratives. As a result, *homo spectaculum* is far more liable to develop incredulity with respect to "ideologies" in general. At the same time, the expressive nature of narrative introduces subjective elements of place and identity into the interpretation of reality. The positive aspect of this loss of meaning is reflected in Habermas's argument that the loss of "real" (universally accepted) meaning providing contexts is an integral step in the development of democratic emancipation. In the work containing his most direct defence of modernity, Habermas asserts that

> the rationalized lifeworld secures the continuity of its contexts of meaning with the discontinuous tools of critique; it preserves the context of social integration by the risky means of an individualistically isolating universalism; and it sublimates the overwhelming power of the genealogical nexus into a fragile and vulnerable universality by means of an extremely individualized socialization. The more abstractly the differentiated structures of the lifeworld operate in the ever more particularized forms of life, the more the rational potential of action oriented toward reaching understanding evolves solely by these means. (Habermas 1987a, p. 346)

Here Habermas implies that the more we exchange the overarching normative orientations of society in favour of individually differentiated and experienced lifeworlds the more we are forced to coordinate action through the pursuit of communicative action. Hence, the more *homo spectaculum* becomes devolved from a social lifeworld and integrated into its systemic peculiarities, the more the opportunity exists to coordinate understanding and action entirely through communicative action. Just as the extension of the franchise was a positive step forward because it forced communicative engagement despite the loss of intersubjectivity it entailed, Habermas believes that this increasing detachment from a specific cultural lifeworld should also be viewed as a positive step. The loss of a shared lifeworld means that legitimacy might increasingly demand the discursive redemption of claims to truth. Even though it makes communicative agreement a little harder to achieve, the detachment from the lifeworld brings with it an expanded capacity for communicative action.

Habermas can therefore be understood to be optimistic about the impact of this loss of ideology upon culture, insofar as it allows for a more personally legitimate and satisfying integration between self and world. In the contemporary world, however, we tend to find that disagreements about truth are more often settled through a redistribution of steering media than through communicative action. Because of the materialist ramifications of a political public realm dominated by *homo faber* we find that material has more public salience than agreement. For Habermas this means that the lifeworld tends towards colonisation under the conditions of instrumental thought. The way to avoid this tendency is to tackle legitimacy at the level of communication itself. He is looking for a change in the basic requirements of communication; not only to ensure that action can be coordinated effectively, but also to ensure that communication takes place. Thus, Habermas and Arendt conclude that it is only by generating significant increases in the levels of participation and access to meaningful communication that the lifeworld can regain its integrity.

This point of agreement between Habermas and Arendt suggests that human emancipation involves allowing all people to tell their story and have it heard. Habermas's emphasis on the discursive redemption of truth claims is nicely complemented by Arendt's emphasis on storytelling as an intersubjective communicative device[5]. Both Habermas and Arendt emphasise that a commitment to pursuing understanding is integral to an inclusive and ideal public. Their view that the act of telling stories simultaneously exposes and validates the self, leads both of them to refuse to validate the philosophical merits of the individual's detachment from the real world and to emphasise public communication as the primary corrective to violence and injustice.

Given the proliferation of petit narratives under the condition of postmodernism, it is possible to contend that the loss of public meaning actually increases the emancipatory potential of a well designed democratic forum. The modern impetus to design such a forum arises from the inevitability of modernity's impact on the world and a normative duty to facilitate the debate about that impact in the most reasonable way possible. The postmodern appeal of such a forum is that it is an attempt to reinstitute critical debate as a form of public self validation. The valorisation of our lifeworld through storytelling not only resists systemic colonisation but furnishes an opportunity to found new understandings in a fragmented world. Alternatively, as Arendt may lead us to believe, the flourishing of democratic public spaces may actually lead us to rediscover the relationship between humans and the world.

Optimistic Impressions of the Impact of Digital Media on the Public Sphere

Deliberative Theory

Habermas himself has been reluctant to engage with the communicative potential of new information and communication technologies. He has, in brief comments, alluded to the fact that the internet has the capacity to foster democratic resistance against authoritarian regimes and that the internet has "reactivated the grassroots of an egalitarian public" (Habermas 2006). However, he maintains that the internet also carries the threat of fragmenting publics into a huge number of isolated issue publics, which, as suggested in Chapter Five, undermines the truly plural nature of the public realm. Nevertheless, many other deliberative theorists have taken up the challenge of applying the principles of ideal communication to digital media. What follows is a summary of the factors concerning digital media which tend to cause optimism amongst these deliberative theorists.

According to deliberative democratic theory, optimism about the democratic potential of the age of the spectacle comes in the form of the communicative evolution of the public sphere. In his work *The Reconstruction of Historical Materialism* Habermas outlines how Marx misjudged the driving force of social progress (Habermas 1976). Habermas argues that it is development in the means of communication, rather than development in the means of production, that is the engine of human history[6]. This is explained in his theory of communicative action in terms of the manner in which social progress is controlled by steering media; strategic control over areas of cultural reproduction translates to the ability to extend systemic influence over the lifeworld (Habermas 1976, p. 267). Habermas understands emancipation in terms of the critical access individuals have to substantive deliberation, and it is this understanding that underlies his emphasis on communicative action as a tool of emancipation. Thus, whereas Marx argues that the engine of social change is control over the means of production, Habermas insists that control over the means of communication is the basic tool of human freedom.

As was suggested in the third chapter, in *The Structural Transformation of the Public Sphere* Habermas argues that it is the development of a critical exchange of information that causes the rise of the emancipatiory public sphere, rather than developments in the mode of production. In his view, "the capitalist mode of production is of course decisive for the *developmental dynamic* that explicates the contents and functions of civil law, but not the *developmental logic* which alone explicates the form and structures of rationality of civil law" (Habermas 1976, p. 267). While Habermas acknowledges that production might affect communication, the key to emancipation remains in the process of communication itself. So, if we are to conduct a search for the structural changes that might bring about emancipation in a Habermasian sense, it is essential that the search concentrates upon those who appropriate and control communication, as opposed to production.

The development of the internet is important in this context, as it has several attributes that can be viewed positively in the light of Habermas's view that communication is the basic element of progress. As a communicative structure the internet has arguably more "ideal" qualities than any previously encountered communications system. Indeed, it is plausible to suggest that the critical potential of humanity has been effectively harnessed in the development of a system of instantaneous and predominantly egalitarian communication. The internet presents a communicative structure that enables an unprecedented amount of communication to take place, removing the physical constraints associated with including massive amounts of participation in debate.

In terms of the critical capacities of democratic systems, the most immediately gratifying outcome of the development of the internet is the access it gives to critical voices. The internet has been described as a rhizomatic form of communication. A rhizome, as described by Deleuze and Guattari, is a network of connected nodes with no centralised features or system of administration (Deleuze & Guattari 1987, pp. 3-25). This "clover-like" structure of the internet can be usefully compared to more traditional "arborescent" (or "tree-like") forms of communication where information must pass through centralised nodes of control before being dispersed. So, where mass media such as newspapers and television broadcasts require centralised collection, filtering and dissemination of information, the internet allows any server the same "publishing" power as any other server. Every node acts both as a potential receiver and transmitter of information. Hence, unlike previous media where the bandwidth for broadcast is finite, the internet is a potentially infinite site of public discussion. Because the internet is conceptually limitless the legal and realistic potential for regulation or censorship of content is undermined (McIntosh & Cates 1998, p. 95). The internet therefore extends the possible public space like never before.

Certainly, the early history of the internet is replete with examples of how the decentralised, pervasive and unedited characteristics of new information and communications technology has contributed to a new lease of life for critical politics. For example, the 1998 Indonesian anti-Suharto uprising was coordinated via digital technology, where the proponents could organise effectively free from the persecution that might have been manifest with actual public appearance (Dalpino 2001). Similarly, whilst the US military attempted to vet the emergence of critical media in the US during the Iraqi invasion of 2004, the internet allowed critical media, such as Al Jazeera, to offer a critical counterpoint not only for the Iraqis but also for citizens of the "Coalition of the Willing". Furthermore, websites undermined the US military's attempt to control the dissemination of sensitive information such as the number of Iraqi civilian casualties resulting from the invasion[7]. The existence and accessibility of these critical voices are a testament to a paradigmatic change in the way in which information can be controlled, and the access individuals have to communication.

At the same time, the bodiless "neutrality" of virtual space offers the prospect that arguments are judged purely on their reasonableness; for virtual space is, in a sense, conducive to intersubjectivity and the discursive redemption of claims to truth[8]. In terms of communicative action, meaning is largely determined not by the force of appearance or the use of money or power, but through the cooperative search for truth and understanding. The internet is the first communication platform to offer the possibility for creating an international public space that is theoretically equitable, inclusive and open.

The commitment to communicative action, as opposed to strategic action, is generated on two counts. Firstly, as mentioned above, the interlocutor must generate success through being understood. Secondly, the abstract qualities of the internet prohibit many strategic gambits from emerging, or being useful, in the course of communication. There is no force aside from the force of the better argument. This encourages "speakers" to say what they truly mean and provides a forum where participation and contributions are difficult to coerce. Thus, the chief goal of interlocutors tends to be achieving understanding, not only because of the inescapable transience of their subjectivity, but also because of the practical difficulty of convincing someone to carry out a course of action through strategic coercion.

Even though the way that the internet is used might not currently reflect the practices that would constitute an ideal public, the development of the infrastructure alone is a quantum leap forward in terms of the creation of inclusive publics. Further, the emergence of the internet has certainly enabled the proliferation of participants in a manner that undermines central authority and control. In the context of Habermas's theory of communicative progress the development of such infrastructure can be perceived to be a good thing for the fostering of critical inputs in a democratic society. In these fundamental ways the internet seems conducive to the kind of ideal conditions that seemed only theoretically possible when Habermas wrote *The Theory of Communicative Action*. While the expansion of trade and communication through the internet may have systemically imperialist implications—the internet certainly linguistifies the sacred and rationalises the lifeworld—the process has also generated a new kind of communication that presents new possibilities for critical interaction with the world. In *The Structural Transformation of the Public Sphere* Habermas claimed that the development of the bourgeois critical public space was an unforeseen by-product of the increasing trade amongst nobles (Habermas 1989, p. 43). It is equally plausible to suggest that the expansion of digital communication in pursuit of profit may once again lead to the emergence of a critical public discourse which has the power to fundamentally alter the common practice of politics.

Agonistic Theory

For agonistic theorists, new information and communication technologies generate significant excitement insofar as these technologies allow for a more personal and expressive engagement between the individual and the world. As noted by Streck, involvement in an internet discussion can be an engaging and self validating experience.

> As in life, identity in cyberspace is cumulative; each contribution a person makes to the interactions of a given group will also contribute to that person's identity within the group, becoming part of the greater whole. Those individual contributions come to be judged not individually but rather in the context of that whole. An inflammatory statement made from a user with a history of calm and rational discourse, for example, will be received much differently than that same statement coming from one with a reputation for hostility. In cyberspace, then, as is the case everywhere people interact, individuals build histories, they develop reputations. Reputation, moreover, as much as race, class and gender can become the basis for distinction. (Streck 1998, p. 39)

Insofar as internet publics provide a forum for revelation, they serve to indulge the agonistic drives of individuals. In doing so, they foster critical thought about issues and about identity itself. By allowing people to become known solely through their commonly received communicative acts, the internet may well be the closest approximation to Arendt's ideal public sphere since the decline of Athens.

The most enthusiastic advocates of the agonistic virtues of digital media have suggested that the rise of the internet—and virtual worlds in particular—will transform the way we live because of digital media's ability to foster our expressive engagement. One of these advocates, Michael H Goldhaber, suggests that digital technology and the profusion of information it produces has given rise to an "attention economy" where attention, rather than material, has become the primary basis of value. In the society of the spectacle, where the vast majority of citizens are excessively materially comfortable, the need for entertainment and personal engagement becomes the primary concern of the individual. Goldhaber points out:

> it is no coincidence that some of the most popular uses of computers, fax machines, networks, phone systems, etc., have more to do with getting attention than with directly aiding what they are supposedly about, increasing productivity of an organisation or society as a whole. (Goldhaber 1997)

Here we see an occlusion of the values of *homo faber* by those of *homo spectaculum*. Insofar as *homo spectaculum* chooses to attach meaning to direct personal expression rather than through reified material expression it is possible to see the emergence of digital communication as a boon for agonism. As we identify our happiness as linked to our expressive engagement rather than our material possessions, our inclination to use that engagement critically and politically should increase.

The idea that contemporary citizens will act upon this agonistic fervour to change the functioning of real publics is taken up by Edward Castronova in his book *Exodus to the Virtual World*. Castronova highlights how effectively digital spaces—particularly those of Massive Multiplayer Online Role Playing Games (MMORPGs)—are able to harness the agonism of their users (Castronova 2007). He points out that these digital spaces are designed so that those who engage with them are met with the precisely appropriate amount of interest, challenge, success and mystery to encourage the user to engage further. The direct public benefit of such engagement is questionable, as once again it appears as if agonism is once again being usurped by private space acting as public space. However, Castronova argues that individuals who become used to this level of engagement will soon become frustrated with the ossified and detached nature of real life public forums and demand a more gratifying relationship with the political system (Castronova 2007). The reflexive and expressive nature of digital media has encouraged a revival of an understanding of the importance of agonism in determining happiness. Through attaching value to personal expression and engagement, *homo spectaculum* has more potential to be meaningfully politically engaged than *homo faber* or *animal laborans*.

As mentioned in the beginning of this chapter, it is only through a synthesis of deliberative and agonistic theories that a critical democratic theory stands to repair democracy. The desire to engage and display, which agonists consider so important, only works within digital technology if communicators respect the conditions of ideal speech. Similarly, the endless deliberation of deliberative democracy is only *realised* if communicators wish to reconcile their virtual worlds with the real world; a wish which is generated by agonism. As can be seen by the development of web technology, there are signs that this synthesis is occurring.

A Positive Synthesis: Spectacular Citizens in a World of Web X.0

Fragmentation of Space

In accordance with the optimism of various theorists about the agonistic and deliberative benefits of digital spaces, there is also growing evidence that individuals are coming to appreciate the democratic nature of the internet. This is perhaps best exemplified by the increasing interactivity of internet technology. The identifying features of what has come to be known as Web 2.0 technology are essentially a technical description of the conditions of the ideal public sphere; they include:

- **User-centred Design**—the Web is designed in a way that is easy and intuitive for all to use, ensuring the greatest degree of inclusivity.

- **Crowd-sourcing**—gathering information from as many places as possible and most importantly, directly from those who use the medium.
- **Web as Platform**—allowing the important processes to be conducted onsite or via the Web application, meaning equal access and lessening the "digital divide".
- **Collaboration**—the principle of sharing and working together as producing the best possible results—with dividends in coverage, participation and objectivity.
- **Power Decentralisation**—a corollary of collaboration, this means that the interaction is not administered but rather automatic. Automatic and consistent service, regardless of client, ensures equal access and interaction.
- **Dynamic Content**—that the content should change over time, according to use and events and it should be particularly responsive to the activities and expressions of the user.
- **Rich User Experience**—a commitment towards ensuring that the user feels validated through the experience of using the space.[9]

These conditions can be understood as a technological simulation of the conditions of an agonistic and deliberative public sphere. The emphasis on power decentralisation, collaboration and user-centred design fulfils deliberative requirements of ideal speech—namely inclusion and deliberation for the sake of a more comprehensive engagement. Similarly, the emphasis on a rich user experience and having dynamic, responsive content follows an agonistic understanding of the virtues of public expression.

The most interesting thing about the evolution of the Web, however, is that it is a response to the desires of *homo spectaculum.* Individuals, companies and groups have sought to alter their internet browsing experiences in these ways. It is possible that the Web lends itself to these kinds of interactions; Tim Berners-Lee, the original creator of the World Wide Web has suggested that Web 2.0 is simply a realisation of what the Web "was always intended to be" (Berners-Lee 2006). Nevertheless, it is also possible to see the evolution of the Web as the product of individuals who are choosing to engage with their reality in the most and expressive and legitimate way possible. If the evolution of the Web continues to validate users' agonism and open up forums for deliberation, we may expect the Web to evolve as an ideal forum for public and political engagement.

There are a number of characteristics of the internet which foster agonistic deliberation. For instance, the "publics" created on the internet are more reflective of the material political conditions within which citizens find themselves. Rather than being constrained to territories defined by their physical boundaries, digital public spaces can encompass the actual territorialities of those engaged in discussion. Hence the internet has been conducive to developing united and intercultural alliances on international issues such as labour and environmental standards. What is perhaps most revolutionary about this development is that it indicates that critique has the infrastructure to follow capital, so that deliberation can mediate the otherwise monopolistic power of capital.

Whilst capital, corporations and big business have developed globally to overcome incommensurabilities, the internet allows communication and critique to achieve the same global spread. For instance, when Nestlé were seen to violate principles of marketing by promoting their baby milk formula in developing countries as safer and better than breastfeeding, an international campaign to boycott Nestlé products was conducted via the internet[10]. Without the internet, Nestlé would have had a far greater chance of controlling the dissemination of information regarding their marketing practices, and they would have also had a greater chance of limiting the need to respond to that information. Internet technology, however, ensures that people are able to be informed about such issues; they are able to respond and they are able to do so in a way which is immanent to the world in which they find themselves. "Technopolitics thus helps labour create global alliances in order to combat increasingly transnational corporations" (Kellner 2001, p. 20). By reflecting the fluid and not necessarily "nationally formed" subjectivities of citizens, the internet provides a malleable public sphere that can respond elegantly and appropriately to contemporary political issues in a deliberative way.

Also, the internet presents itself as an ideal public sphere because it enables personal interaction with a plurality of public spaces. As agonistic theory indicates, the ideal democratic system must be one in which the political choices one makes are immanent to the public in which they are made. This has the benefit of keeping participation in discussions immediate rather than representative, with the resultant requisites for action and possibility of acclaim. Similarly, following his encounter with Nancy Fraser, Habermas has conceded that a single public sphere is no longer as ideal as multiple public spheres each operating as discursive democracies[11]. The benefit of plural, competing and overlapping publics lies both in the level of engagement and response that these publics afford and their ability to be designed around communities rather than geographies. It is possible to enter into public debate on the internet on any topic conceivable; if a forum does not yet exist, it is within the power of any individual to create one. The forum may be extended to include anyone and possibly everyone, but due to the nature of choice, is generally accessed by those with an interest in the forum topic. The resultant discussion is focused, deliberative and, in a practical sense, eternal. The decentred yet pervasive quality of the internet caters for multiple yet immanent publics in a way that was previously difficult to materially constitute.

Fragmentation of Individuals

The issue of the fragmentation of public space ought to remind us of the fragmentation of the individual with which this has been associated. While the detrimental effects of the loss of the individual are highlighted in chapters Four and Six, there are also reasons to be positive about the fragmented subjectivity of *homo spectaculum*. The major reason for optimism is that through undermining the dominance of one particular space of engagement the Web has undermined the dominance of any particular form of rationality. Through the nature of this fragmentation, it's possible to see a benefit for agonistic deliberation insofar as the authority of tradition and the tradition of authority have been set communicatively aflow. In the absence of universal rules, we ask ourselves what is right more often in a way that requires thought, rather than knowledge. With the aforementioned incredulity towards the substance of *homo faber's* instrumental claims to rationality, the process of identity formation may take place with a much greater degree of thoughtfulness.

The concept that the new individual has critical potential was explored by Jean-Francois Lyotard before the technological development of the internet. Lyotard anticipated that the decline of grand narratives would produce more elaborately critical and empowered individuals (Lyotard 1984). He argued that we can no longer view science, production or anything else as the driving force of progress. In terms of rationality, we have, in a sense, progressed beyond the point where such stories could be *useful*[12]. This has created a situation where legitimacy becomes defined on a much more subjective scale, and comes to rest upon the narrative structures surrounding the subject. In the process, as individuals we become more acutely aware of our role in constituting the narratives which we deem legitimate. We thus engage with our own lifeworld in such a way that is continuous and contingent upon our own actions—which is a boon to both our own agonistic expression and our ability to critically deliberate. As can be seen in digital media effects models, this is expressly clear when dealing with new communications technology such as the internet.

Information and communications technology has opened up new possibilities for participation in identity forming contexts; and as Poster argues, "by directly tinkering with reality, a simulational practice is set in place which forever alters the conditions under which the identity of the self is formed" (Poster 1994, p. 79). The new constitution of subjectivity can thus be understood to promote a dialogue between "myself and I". In seeking to recapture identity, one seeks to relate various spaces to each other in ways which create flows between them. In seeking to express themselves through actions that control flows and alter them even infinitesimally, a subject tends to seek to reconcile their various selves towards one coherent whole. This practice of reconciliation comes to represent Arendt's conception of "thinking" far more elaborately than the previous "colonising" effects media has had on subject formation.

The combined effect of fragmented spaces and fragmented individuals is that there are more opportunities than ever for self-expression and deliberation. Ideally, these acts of expressing and deliberating can also produce public dividends. One example of how such a dividend can be produced is micro-financing. Micro-financing thrives upon the meta-geographical spread of the internet to allow those with money to make small investment loans to those without money. This is a decentred, collaborative and non-heirarchical approach to finance but it does nothing without a public to support it. But *homo spectaculum*, checking their social networking site, can witness that a friend of theirs has made a loan to a dressmaker, who wishes to buy a sewing machine with the investment. Despite the fact the dressmaker lives in a place geographically, culturally and politically isolated from *homo spectaculum*, they can empathise with the dressmaker's plight and orient themselves towards achieving a result which is profitable for both of them. So *homo spectaculum* lends the dressmaker some money, for a very marginal lending rate, which allows the dressmaker to increase their productivity. As *homo spectaculum* does so, a message is automatically posted to their social networking portfolio, announcing the action they have taken and providing *homo spectaculum* with validation in the process. Such machines are already in operation for the purposes of commerce and while there are very few such machines with explicitly political expressions, there are reasons to think these will arise. They can certainly be created.

Democracy as Resistance

Finally, one of the major reasons for being optimistic about the emergence of a new vital public sphere from the shackles of the ossified representative system is that ideal democratic practice has always flourished at the precise moments when it has suffered the threat of supression. Arendt identifies the ideal democratic natures of revolutionary councils, resistance groups and soviets, which sprung up precisely because there was no political outlet for agonistic deliberation. "Each time they appeared", she states, "they sprang up as spontaneous organs of the people, not only outside of all revolutionary parties but entirely unexpected by them and their leaders" (Arendt 1990, p. 249). Similarly, Habermas's ideal public sphere of the critical bourgeois meeting in public houses to discuss public issues arose largely because these public deliberators understood their power was otherwise ineffectual. In all these cases, the overbearing awareness of the lost power to express one's opinion and to have these opinions matter was the source of the founding of a new public. And in each of these cases, an awareness of the benefits of inclusion and participation formed the basis of the ideal public.

It is possible to believe that reality and identity seeking individuals may take the opportunity to produce an ideal democratic public sphere. Elements of such a public sphere are springing up now, evidenced in the development of web technology to become more egalitarian, and cater more towards the expression and deliberation of individuals. While politicians have made token gestures towards exploiting the advertising potential of this technology, for the most part, they have failed to embrace its democratic potential. As a result, it is possible to see that the expressive and deliberative elements of digital technology serve to increase frustration with the archaic nature of representative democracy.

Moreover, as suggested by theorists such as Mark Poster and internet optimists such as John Perry Barlow, Howard Rheingold and Henry Jenkins, digital technology has a degree of determinism which resists the constructions of individuals as *homo faber*. According to these theories, digital spaces function as places of difference from and resistance to modern society.

> In a sense, they serve the function of a Habermasian public sphere, however reconfigured, without intentionally or even actually being one. They are places not of the presence of validity claims or the actuality of critical reason, but of the inscription of new assemblages of self-constitution. (Poster 1997, p. 224)

According to this understanding, digital technologies reinsert consciousness into the process of meaning creation. The role of the individual in determining the world with which they choose to engage requires a critical exchange between self and world which is not simply determined by a single overarching public form of reason. This exchange is inherently communicative, as it is motivated by a person seeking an identity that has integrity and, in turn, it precipitates a need for a community that gives a more immediate sense of reality. Such a synthesis points to the ways in which information and communication technologies can foster the development of a critical and engaging public space amongst the very public that needs it the most—the society of the spectacle.

The idea that *homo faber* has somehow already won, that we cannot possibly break the hold of economic rationality over public life, ignores the evidence that there is a growing dissatisfaction with that public life which is manifesting alternative public spheres at an unprecedented rate. In the emergence of social networking sites, wikis, discussion boards, blogs and massive multiplayer online games we can see the beginnings of a new public sphere which has the potential to highlight the one dimensionality of representative democracy. At the same time we now have *homo spectaculum*, a type of citizen who has come to expect responsiveness, to learn to negotiate meaning and to assume expression as a right. These things suggest that the Age of the Spectacle could truly produce a spectacular form of democracy, despite representative democracy's claim to be all powerful.

> At the end of the feudal period, the pomp and display of the nobility reached a level never before attained; the most gorgeous armor, the most magnificent tournaments of knights, the most elaborate ceremonies between rival nobles, the most brilliant marriages, the greatest interest in noble lineage. But by then it had lost all real function or importance. So today, when the stock market goes up and up, when money wealth itself seems a source of fame more than ever, when being number one on Forbes 400 list seems the height of perfection, when every basketball superstar wants a contract that is at least a million more than the last record one, we seem to be more dazzled by money than ever, just as we seem to be more intrigued by material goods than ever. But these interests are superficial and faddish. They are signs of decadence not of a glorious future for the money economy. Even in themselves they speak to the growing desire for attention, the need for it as well. Money is now little more than numbers, one number among many, and as a source of lasting attention it can fade in an instant. The attention economy is already here, and more completely so every day. (Goldhaber 1997)

It is precisely at the point that a system assumes its inherent supremacy that it neglects to seek to justify itself and it presents the possibility that it will be undermined by its ever more tenuous claims to legitimacy. In these instances the lifeworld can strike back.

What Can Be Done?

> This is my world
> And I am the world leader pretend
> This is my life
> And this is my time
> I have been given the freedom
> To do as I see fit
> It's high time I've razed the walls
> That I've constructed
>
> —REM 'World Leader Pretend' (1989)

The hallmark of a successful democracy lies in its ability to provide its citizens with the opportunity to partake in meaningful public engagement over shared resources and decisions. This book has sought to outline how far away from this engagement the democracies of late capitalism are and to highlight how this shortcoming is affecting public action. This outline of the myopic development of contemporary public spaces is not intended to imply that there is no hope for humanity, but to generate awareness of this situation so that these issues can be considered when constructing new democratic institutions. Habermas's and Arendt's theories can be useful in this context. A combination of their theories enables a characterisation of liberal democracies as inherently flawed *in the way they reflect individual sovereignty.*

In highlighting how contemporary conditions restrain emancipative development I hope to encourage readers to act—to utilise the expressive action of one's own, which, according to Habermas and Arendt, is really the only hope for recapturing a sense of self-rule. My method has thus been in the realm of traditional critical theory—to create an awareness of what is wrong in order to generate a motivation to make things right. If I have emphasised the trouble we are in, it is only because nothing will change without the conscious motivation to act. As Gregory Bateson has identified "the experience of defeat not only serves to convince [us] that change is necessary: it is the first step to change" (Bateson 1987, p. 313).

By describing the emergence of *homo spectaculum* I am instrumentalising my own understanding of Habermas and Arendt in order to highlight how deliberative and agonistic democratic theories apply to contemporary conditions. In doing so I have refrained from focusing upon the timeless applicability of their solutions to problems in favour of focusing on diagnosing the specific problem with contemporary democratic function. In part, I want to reground optimism about the inherent positive characteristic of new technologies and new modes of being. In their manifesto for political change *Empire* (2000), Hardt and Negri suggest that a revolutionary "multitude" might be formed through an autonomous process of critical engagement with the contradictions of the age of the spectacle (Hardt & Negri 2000). What Hardt and Negri lack is a depiction of how this subjectivity might be engaged, given the overwhelming colonisation of the lifeworld as it exists. Whilst the theoretical basis for optimism may be warranted, and perhaps they don't want to jeopardise the appeal of their vision with concreteness, I feel their optimism with respect to the potential of the multitude is misplaced if it is not preceded by a change in the way political deliberation takes place.

The first step towards reinvigorating democratic citizenship is to understand that the problems with democracy arise from a lack of citizen engagement. The democratic system doesn't fail because politicians are inherently corrupt, or because the system is designed to fail, the democratic system fails because it does not engage the common citizen in the process of democracy. A lack of critical engagement with public issues is one of the most concerning side effects of this lack of engagement, but we may also see the development of an overly consumptive waste economy as attributable to the lack of expressive public engagement. The immediate task for any attempt to stem this development is to begin celebrating the personal and public benefits of citizens participating in political processes.

From agonistic theory we learn that political participation ought to be direct–not representative. As a result, ideal decision making forums need to be small enough to facilitate such direct participation and they need to be open and flexible in order to encourage engagement. From deliberative theory we learn that political discussions ought to be oriented primarily toward achieving understanding, that the basic conditions of participation is that you are committed to explaining your position until you are understood. Small, local political organisations which abide by the conditions of ideal communication are, in principle, the most democratic. However, beyond these broad ideals which should guide the composition of democratic forums, there are more specific prescriptions which can be used to democratise different realms of action.

For *animal laborans* the task is to grant access to the decision making processes which govern the uses of, and profit derived from, labour. The problem with the act of labour is that it denies the labourer the opportunity to take part in the acts of expressing, debating and deciding, which would allow the labourer to become engaged in the work in which they take part. One solution to this issue is to avoid the development of jobs where labour does not have some kind of representation in the management of that labour. Trade unions and guilds are historical examples of attempts to institutionalise such representation but these are typically banned in the sweatshops and manufacturing sectors of the developing world. For such people, access to digital communications technology could provide an anonymous avenue for communication within otherwise banned workers' organisations. Furthermore, the ability to spread information and attract global attention could empower such organisations to play a greater role in determining who manufactures which products and how those products are received in an international market.

For *homo faber*, the task is to ensure that work is made more expressive and to give workers a greater awareness of the relationship between their work and what it produces on a public scale. The worst aspects of instrumental thinking—as evidenced in Eichmann's concentration camps, the development of a waste economy and the bankers' pursuit of profit over public accountability—are all products of people working too hard towards goals that are ill-considered. The solution to this problem is to increase the relationship between the company and the community. It is important to celebrate efforts of business to consider the "triple bottom line", meaning the impact of work upon people and the planet, as well as profit. While there can be no doubt that many of these gestures by companies are spectacles designed purely to incresase profit, making these claims means we can hold them accountable. Furthermore, there are good business reasons for overcoming the detachment of the system of work from the lifeworld. In a post-scarcity world, productivity ought not be the only criteria of success. The more a company can include and relate to the lifeworld of its workers and its market, the greater it will be able to use consensual norms to facilitate action, rather than relying on money and power. Re-inserting the practice of consideration as an element of fabrication will not only correctly orient organisations, it will also empower and motivate workers, while improving the quality and social contribution of their products.

It is in the rise of *homo spectaculum* that we can see the potential for encouraging *homo faber* and *animal laborans* to become more involved in public life. *Homo specatculum* has surpassed the realm of necessity which made instrumentalism such a compelling component of industrialisation and has learnt the value of expression as an element of well-being. Armed with these qualities *homo spectaculum* is uniquely equipped to engage with democratic practices.

Given the progress the market has made in engaging the agonism of consumers, the primary task for democratic reform must be to develop democratic practices which are equally as engaging. Digital technology offers an overwhelming series of possibilities in this regard and while governments are generally reluctant to open up democratic deliberation to the public, there has been some very gentle progress in this direction. Rather than relying on conscientious citizens to redeem democracy, we must use democracy to re-engage conscientious citizenship. One spectacular way to jump-start an awareness of the importance of democratic engagement would be to merge democratic campaigns with reality television. As the spectacle surrounding democratic elections becomes ever more stage-managed and less and less interesting, we find that citizens are left unsure of candidates' real identities and attitudes. What better way to bind the publicity driven campaigns to actual public scrutiny than to place all candidates in a *Big Brother*-like reality television series which places political candidates under a public spotlight and portrays their responses to public issues away from their spin doctors and image managers.

The formula could work something like this: place all candidates in a constantly surveilled environment. To get a glimpse of their real, consistent identity, take the opportunity to place them under situations of conflict and stress and ask them to answer a series of questions about policies and personal beliefs; questions which can be continually submitted by viewers using SMS technology. The nation votes one candidate out of contention weekly until two candidates remain, at which point a normal electoral ballot can be pursued. While reality television is certainly open to the charge that it is not particularly "real", it is at least as genuine as the stage-managed media appearances and scripted debates which currently dominate election coverage. More importantly, such participation in mass media would reinvigorate public interest in political representatives and political processes. Just as *Big Brother* created instant celebrity for its participants and as reality television involving dancing and cooking have raised public interest in these pursuits, the elevation of politics to a blatant spectacle would surely increase the profile of, and interest in, political processes.

There are problems with this idea; the power of television producers to shape perceptions of candidates would be overwhelming and the whole exercise could descend into mindless populism. Of course, these problems reflect the current issues surrounding the media's ability to operate as a "kingmaker" and, in an important sense, a *Political Big Brother* would draw attention to these issues. Furthermore, some consideration of ideal communication could allow the production of such media to take place with a principle of balance intact. One solution would be to ensure that people are able to compile their own production of the show from live digital feeds on the internet, another would be to allow each political party to produce their own summary of each day's events. In this way, the integration of media production with political process can draw attention to the fact that our democracy is mediated through mass media. Done well, such a move could reinvigorate interest in politics and raise the public's concerns about democratic processes; and it wouldn't take much for such a program to be put in place as it wouldn't necessarily require constitutional change.

There are, of course, more extreme constitutional reforms which would increase the democratic nature of spectacular citizenship. Many of these possibilities relate to the idea of universalising democratic rights (inclusion in deliberation and decision making) as applicable to every aspect of an individual's world. One such strategy would be to extend the franchise to reflect the extension of the market. That is, to change the nature of the rights of affiliation so that participation in the market can be seen as carrying with it the right to deliberate over and vouch for the legitimacy of the private decisions made by market participants. This level of consumer involvement is difficult to reconcile with the private-interest operation of capitalism and yet it need not be antithetical to capitalist development. Indeed, as mentioned earlier, many private companies are suggesting that they appreciate a reciprocal relationship with their customers; a measure such as consumer citizenship would simply institutionalise this relationship.

The central element of consumer citizenship is that citizens' democratic rights extend to consumption. The rights considered are essentially the rights to engage with any private organisation in a communicative interaction which approaches the norms of ideal speech (that is, being inclusive, deliberative and oriented to reaching understanding). As such, a purchaser of a product would instantly be awarded with a fundamental right to obtain and question any and all information regarding the manufacture, transportation and marketing of that product. The consumer is, at the same time, entitled to make arguments about how these processes may be improved and to expect that their suggestions shall be earnestly debated and considered. Through such a mechanism, the consumer has the opportunity to place the requirement of communicative reason upon the producer and undermine some of the more flagrant abuses of consumerism. The consumer actions which would be enabled range from addressing the excessive claims of product advertising to exposing and addressing any unreasonable distribution of company profits. While the political pressure necessary to institutionalise consumer citizenship may be a long way off, it seems that a progressive company may see such consumer participation as a successful and innovative way of marketing and managing their product.

The most promising area of concern regarding the democratic impetus of the age of the spectacle is that *homo spectaculum* has come to expect responsiveness from the spaces with which they engage. At all points the tenets of inclusivity, deliberation and response have been hard-wired into these spaces; and, as discussed in Chapter Seven, they approximate ever more ideal public spaces. The most distressing concern for the public in the age of spectacle is that as many "private" publics do become more ideal, the democratic political system remains unresponsive; an ossifying and decaying fossil of a once vital and inspirational idea. As *homo spectaculum* becomes ever more detached from the instrumental spirit which gave rise to representative democracy, it becomes ever more pressing that the demoratic system undergoes some change.

This book is, in part, an attempt to create the impetus for this change. Even the public realm of *homo faber* concedes to the utility of starting to think about what the human race is going to do about universal concerns such as global warming, depletion of drinking water and rising sea water levels. People who suggest we cannot meaningfully discuss these common problems because we are all too different, essentially recreate the fallacy of the spectacle. The continual appropriation of difference so as to confound the possibility of working together is placing the cart before the horse. We do all share some characteristics—we are all human and we are increasingly facing problems that can only be solved collectively. As such, we find ourselves in a concrete world with opportunities for founding and for clearing a space within which freedom can emerge. If governments do not take advantage of these spaces, they will continue to retain an ever decreasing proportion of the money and power which can be used to implement change. I would suggest everyone in politics can and should use this as a motivation towards regaining legitimacy.

Part of what we learn from Habermas and Arendt then, both through their argument and their action, is that we cannot talk about politics without saying something about ourselves. Even Habermas, who desperately seeks to avoid giving his project any normative slant, relies on some assumptions about legitimacy and humanity in order to generate some purpose to his project. In writing this book I understand that any concept of reality is inherently flawed, but I also understand that it unavoidably affects what we do, so ought to be discussed. Habermas and Arendt merely ask us to reveal our real self, communicate about ourselves and understand ourselves, within the context of the world we create. Against this conception, the liberal argument that the state should leave the individual alone is completely inadequate as a way of conceptualising politics and sovereignty in the digital era. In seeking to find a way to harness our self-expression and validate ourselves; we can also seek to refound our relationship to the world.

The world stands on the edge of a precipice in regard to the major concern of critical theory: universal emancipation. Whilst the means for equitable ideal communication may well have become available to all and we have "post-scarcity" economies, the economic, social and ecological gap between the richer and poorer nations is rapidly increasing. Governments and international organisations look to the expansion of the international market to define value and force political change. In the process the market continues to control communication and install a functional and productive ideology in its place. The ways in which the markets have managed to centralise their international management systems and construct them as public spaces for elites suggests it is not impossible to organise meaningful international cooperation. Markets have done this despite problems with language, customs and values; indeed, they have flourished with energy and innovation derived from these differences.[1]

Because of our collective regard for knowledge and thought (or strategy and communication), economics and politics hold the positions they do in our society. Like Arendt and Habermas I believe that returning politics to its public place is the primary condition for human emancipation insofar as it once again makes thought a public concern. The wellspring for such a task lies in the intrinsic value and legitimacy of communicative power which always exists as a potential antidote to systemic abuses. Opportunities to engage this power are not only available to *homo spectaculum* but are abundant and can be summarised in one principle: public power requires public scrutiny. Although the traditional public spaces in which to do this have been occluded, the system has created some discursive situations that may suffice for this purpose. As Habermas points out, the court of law is largely designed to emulate an ideal speech situation and therefore enables the redress of systemic abuses. In addition we have the internet, an egalitarian communication structure that presents the possibility that communication and political power may be linked in an equitable and accessible way. Finally, even existing systems of government are sometimes required to justify their own legitimacy—particularly in moments of founding such as the emergence of a new republic. At such points there is an opportunity to think anew of how the political system could be improved. All these forums present the opportunity for emancipation but, as I hope this book indicates, they will never be emancipatory forums until we regard them in this way.

Notes

Introduction

1   (Arendt 1970, p. 41) quoted in (Habermas 1983).

2   This was subsequently reprinted in his *Philosophical-Political Profiles* (Habermas 1983).

3   This shared understanding is the very opposite of that of Descartes, who isolated himself from the world in order to determine what was real.

Chapter One: The Agonistic Public Realm

1   Arendt has been accused of being overly sympathetic to Eichmann, in not being able to see his demonic intention in constructing and designing death camps (Kristeva 2001a, p. 145). To her critics she seems to have a misplaced faith that Eichmann would not have been able to carry out these unconscionable acts had he engaged in an internal dialogue; that is, had he started actually *thinking* as opposed to *knowing*. Indeed it may appear that the line Arendt draws between banality and evil serves no other purpose than to stress her own faith in a particular type of non-instrumental thought.

2   The term "realised" highlights how the link between thought and reality, is mediated by public speech and action; to "realise" something is to make it real through consideration and reflection.

3   (Arendt 1958, p. 175) cited in (Kristeva 2001a, p. 171).

4   There is some debate about the accuracy of Arendt's reading as there is some evidence to suggest that the Athenian polis was somewhat hostile to individualism—perhaps best exemplified by the trial of Socrates. However, Arendt certainly paints the polis as a forum for collaborative individualism; convinced by the heroism inspired by the Athenian polis, epitomised by Socrates' defence of the virtue of the polis during his trial.

5   This critique was first described as the "occlusion of the public by the social" in (Benhabib 1990); it has subsequently been discussed by (Pitkin 1998) and (Isaac 1994) among others.

6   For a closer analysis of the rise of the social sphere see (Pitkin 1998).

7   John Sitton has analysed Arendt's predilection towards decentralisation in (Sitton 1987).

8   From a series of Jefferson's personal correspondences; letters 8940–8943 in (Jefferson 1900, p. 921).

9   "Participatory" democracy is not something Arendt directly advocates, due, no doubt, to her "phenomenological essentialism", which leads her to insist that the Christian doctrine of non-engagement deserves the same *a priori* respect as any other privately formed opinion. In a *force de jure* she would insist that the doctrine of non-engagement must be publicly justified before it is publicly accepted as legitimate.

10   Despite their approximation of the virtue of the agonal Greek polis, Arendt notes that modern revolutionary publics have never managed to survive their own founding. She notes disdainfully the capitulation of the thought of these spontaneous public realms in the face of political "knowledge" (Arendt 1990, p. 264). The founding of such a public in

the modern period, although spurred on by a human need to oppose the prevailing public realm, is doomed by the modern conception that reality is constituted prior to the individual. With the dominance of this understanding, the tendency has been for councils to acquiesce in the face of more instrumentally legitimate power structures of administration. Throughout the modern period the victories won through agonistic, participatory democracies have been quickly exploited by experts who "knew" what needed to happen. Since "man has lost faith in himself as partner of his own thoughts", Arendt understands that the moments in which he regains that faith are unique and rare moments—"islands in the sea or oases in the desert" (Arendt 1990, p. 275).

Chapter Two: Deliberative Democracy

1   As readers will recognise, this is a reference to Kant's famous article 'Answering the Question: What is Enlightenment?'(Kant 1985). Similarly *The Theory of Communicative Action* is an attempt to articulate the emancipatory potential of the public use of reason. The following is an attempt to articulate *The Theory of Communicative Action* (Habermas 1984) and (Habermas 1987b) focusing on elements relevant to a study of his theory of democracy.

2   "I count as communicative action those linguistically mediated interactions where all participants pursue illocutionary aims...On the other hand, I regard as linguistically mediated strategic action those interactions in which at least one of the participants wants his speech acts to produce perlocutionary effects on his opposite number" (Habermas 1984, p. 295).

3   See (Habermas 1994) and (Habermas 1987b, pp. 119-152).

4   Such as when participants do not share a common lifeworld and thus do not share unproblematic convictions and understandings.

5   A thorough account of this trial can be found at the website www.mcspotlight.org, or in the publication (Vidal 1997).

6   (Rehg & Bohman 2002, p. 33) citing (Habermas 1984, pp. 1-42 and 273-337).

Chapter Three: Media, Technology and Democracy

1   The strength and loyalty of such fundamentally unengaged private citizens to public symbols indicates a normative proclivity of humanity, that is, a fundamental desire to show normative allegiance. This "creation of meaning" is central to Kant's work "An Old Question Raised Again: Is the Human Race Constantly Progressing?" discussed by Arendt in (Arendt 1982, p. 19) and in Habermas's discussion of Weber (Habermas 1984, p. 187). This proclivity will be further examined in Chapter Four.

2   The invitation to William of Orange to take up the English crown is a good example of this. When England's political and religious leaders sought to change the state's religious system from Catholic to Protestant, they chose to make this move by replacing Catholic James II with the Protestant William of Orange.

3   "The awakened readiness of the consumers involves the false consciousness that as critically reflecting private people they contribute responsibly to public opinion" (Habermas 1989, p. 194).

4   It is interesting that upon his election to Parliament John Stuart Mill railed against this situation, insisting that his election elevated him to best engage in arguments that were good for his constituents, rather than merely representing the aggregated interests of individual constituents.

5   The tragedy of the commons is a dilemma where private people acting in their private interests will degrade and deplete a common resource despite it being clear that the preservation of the resource is in everyone's best interest. The problem arises when what is shared is considered less important than what is personally gained. The tragedy of the commons was first outlined in (Hardin 1968).

6   Much ado has been made by democratic theorists about the bases and consequences of the subsequent differences between agonistic and deliberative democratic systems. My ambition is to highlight the similarities between Habermas's and Arendt's democratic projects, rather than the differences. I have argued that they share an understanding of the communicative composition of power, and of personal sovereignty as the ability to critically engage in this power. To be sure, Habermas emphasises the importance of establishing an ideal mode of communication, while Arendt emphasises the importance of establishing an ideal space for communication, but this does not render their projects to be exclusive of each other.

Chapter Four: Introducing the Age of the Spectacle

1   Debord further describes the society of the spectacle in (Debord 1990).

2   (Marcuse no date) cited in Douglas Kellner's 1991 "Introduction to the Second Edition" of (Marcuse 1964).

3   By "universal meaningful orientations" I am referring to the grand narratives of modernity such as instrumentalism and progress, as well as traditional value systems such as religion and custom.

4   The Nietzchean concept of "eternal recurrence" is that one should live one's life as though everything one did would recur throughout eternity—in this way, one must constantly confront the question of whether one is living a life according to one's own will (Nietzsche 1986). Arendt's assertiveness on this point is noteworthy, considering her heavy emphasis on the dangers of knowing anything.

5   (Villa 2001, p. 23) quoting (Sandel 1982).

6   For example, Mill promotes individuality as being a fundamental component of progress, whereas Arendt is hostile to ideas of progress and promotes individuality insofar as it is an expression of self.

7   Base because such people display as slaves to those who have created the boundaries of their *ressentiment*, rather than as an expression of self.

8   A similar thesis was developed by Jean Baudrillard in (Baudrillard, 1994).

9   This fluidity of capital is enabled by the rise of digital technologies, as explored in (Luke 1998, p. 137).

10 The notion has been developed by (Beniger 1986; Toffler 1990) and (Lyotard 1984) amongst others.

11 Although there is little chance of immortality for *homo spectaculum*—the acclaim of the spectacle is, by its very nature, transient.

Chapter Five: The "Public" Realms of Spectacular Society

1   See, for example (Robert & Dennis 2005) and (Shah et al. 2007).

2   I shall examine this argument in Chapter 7.

3   "There aren't any public parks or libraries in cyberspace—it has all been sold" (McIntosh & Cates 1998, p. 84).

4   I have explored these positive potentials more fully in (Harper 2009) and in Chapter 7 of this book.

5   For a discussion of the relative merits of "cyber salons" in Habermasian terms see (Dean 2001).

6   One notable exception to this rule is the historically important internet community known as the WELL. Realising that the lack of identity was a flaw in using the internet as public space, the WELL community has made it mandatory to maintain a consistent identity whilst participating in WELL discussions, and has sought to reconcile online existence with real world existence through public meetings. While the WELL encapsulates most of the positive possibilities of the internet as public space, it is certainly the exception rather than the rule. See (Wilson 1997, p. 149).

7   The functions the internet provides include communication, commerce, education, information archive and entertainment.

8   For an optimistic appraisal see (Rheingold 1993).

9   Quite literally, as many shopping centres are designed around a transept, similar to the design of medieval cathedrals and understood to convey a certain form of reverent publicness which constrains interaction between people, while maximising their exposure to their surroundings. For a detailed exploration of how shopping centres have usurped the role of churches as providers of meaning, see (Pahl 2004).

10   For a specific study illustrating this see (Abaza 2001).

11   (Williagan 1992, p. 92) cited in (Klein 2000).

12   If we take consumers to be forever attempting to reach an understanding of the world, and accept the cultural transmissions they receive as objectively "real", then they are subject to defining their understandings according to the predefined interests of strategic actors. As Frederick Olafson has noted, liars employ the conventions of communicative action in order to make their lies seem compelling. The only difference between the activity of lying and the activity of communicative action is an earnest commitment to truth, which is surrendered by the presence of a strategic actor (Olafson 1990, p. 653).

13   Marketers typically employ the conventions of communicative action in order to pursue their strategic goals—appearing communicative makes their claims to truth appear more legitimate.

14   Referring to Arendt's statement "Political phenomena emerge into their space from an opaque and impenetrable darkness, which is the human heart. Forever closed to 'scientific' inquiry, it may yet be illuminated by the insight of poets" (Arendt 1971, p. 418).

15   Scott Bedbury, marketing vice-president of Starbucks quoted in *The New York Times*, 20 October 1997 and (Peters 1997, p. 96).

16   Quoting the book's author, Patricia S. Wilson, cited in (Klein 2000, p. 175).

17   This reference may be lost on younger readers as Ponds cosmetics has rebranded itself as a simple, wholesome beauty company, whereas once it presented its beauty products as

breakthrough technology, scientifically researched in the branded "Ponds Institute". At the time of writing, L'Oreal has taken over as the beauty company whose pseudo-scientific posturing is most chilling. See ("Research" 2010) for statements such as "Our challenge is to listen to women and men around the world, and anticipate their dreams".

18   See Chapter 9 "Silent Science—The Corporate Takeover of the Universities" in (Monbiot 2000a).

19   "What is real is what appears as the same to all who behold it" (Arendt 1958, p. 57).

Chapter Six: The Politics of the Spectacle

1   Such as widely facilitated by the "privatisation" of public institutions to allow such institutions to operate under greater market influence.

2   Arendt discusses the thoughtlessness effected by the loss of public meaning in (Arendt 1967, p. 477 esp.).

3   Advertisements for such vehicles seem to invariably depict a fantasy that command over such a vehicle translates to command over the environment around it. As Marcuse suggests and was discussed earlier, for *homo spectaculum* freedom is seen as control over everything (see (Marcuse 1968)).

4   The lack of true public space for disclosure is linked to this inability. The private public spaces of *homo spectaculum* modulate themselves in order to ensure that what is suitable behaviour at one moment is inappropriate in the next.

5   "image-making [has become] global policy" (Arendt 1972, pp. 21, 18) .

6   Of course, the proliferation of air conditioners also degrades the real public by contributing to public heat and depleting public energy resources.

7   I summarised this account of the 2008 Global Financial Crisis from the much more erudite accounts of (Tett 2009a) and (Lanchester 2010).

8   'Majority world' is used to designate what has less accurately been known as the 'third', 'developing' or 'undeveloped' world.

9   Speciation is the point at which a new species evolves from its original and becomes a separate species. The condition of speciation tends to occur when the new and original species will no longer reproduce with each other.

10   See (Marx 1973b, pp. 70-72) for some particularly appropriate comments about how "the bourgeoisie cannot exist without constantly revolutionising the means of production" and how "the need of a constantly expanding market for its products chases the bourgeoisie over the whole surface of the globe. It must nestle everywhere, establish connections everywhere".

11   See also (Ralston Saul 1997), (Soros 1998) and (Monbiot 2003).

12   See (Der Derian 2001) for an exposition on this connection.

13   See, for example, (Olesen 2005).

Chapter Seven: Constructing a Critical Democratic Theory

1   Such as (Mouffe 2000b).

2   Those who appropriate Habermas's deliberative democracy as rationally hegemonic misunderstand the purpose of communicative action. According to such a reading, Habermas's theory of communicative action seems to suggest that we might find that an agreement would render further debate needless if we were all included in processes of decision making. Put this way, if we universally experienced an ideal speech situation and if every citizen of the earth could contribute and come to agreement about existence through the use of communicative action, the result of communication would then be reality defining and somewhat limiting of the possibilities of further thought, criticism and distinction. An Arendtian perspective on the inevitable plurality of the world, however, asserts that the natural world will always contribute the unexpected, local variances and other plural inconsistencies that would generate rupture and disagreement. Habermas himself is acutely aware of the local nature of legitimacy, hence his focus on communicatively constituted legitimacy as opposed to universal truth.

3   This position was perceived to be a weakness by Habermas who lauds Arendt's conception of communicative power and critical publicity but criticises Arendt for retreating "into the tradition of natural right." rather than justifying democracy on an abstract notion of communicative legitimacy (Habermas 1983, p. 185).

4   While the term "petite narratives" is intended to invoke Lyotard's understanding of the postmodern challenge to grand narratives (Lyotard 1984), I am consciously using the feminine "petite" rather than "petit" to indicate that much of this hope springs not just from the rise of small stories but the rise of those stories which have previously been marginalised.

5   The central role of narrative in Arendt's work is explored by Julia Kristeva (Kristeva 2001b), (Kristeva 2001a).

6   Habermas's emphasis on the use of communication as an emancipatory force, as opposed to Marx's emphasis on material production, is explored in (Owen 2002).

7   Such as www.iraqbodycount.net

8   A positive interpretation of the bodiless virtues of cyberspace in terms of the work of Habermas and Arendt can be found in (Saco 2002, p. 37 especially).

9   For elaboration on this list see (Sharma 2008)

10   For more information concerning this campaign see
http://www.babymilkaction.org/pages/boycott.html

11   For Fraser's contribution of "multiple publics" see (Fraser 1992); for Habermas's discussion with Fraser see (Calhoun 1992, pp. 462-481). Habermas's concession to multiple publics can be seen as reflecting his theoretical shift from consensus establishing truth (objective reality) to consensus establishing legitimacy (dependent upon a shared lifeworld).

12   As poet Muriel Rukeyser describes it, we are more aware that "The Universe is made of stories, not of atoms". For those seeking a "unified theory of everything" the contemporary emergence of "string theory" in physics defies atomistic conceptions of the universe and tells us what narrative theorists have always said—the universe is built upon transcendental threads that vary reality through modulation.

Conclusion: What Can Be Done?

1   Certainly what makes the market so successful in this regard is that it does not have to legitimate itself continuously through communicative power. Rather than pursuing agreement through reason, the market can neutralise disagreement through the judicious use of money and power. Unfortunately, this same characteristic prohibits the market from being a thoughtful, legitimate or emancipatory means for coordinating action.

Bibliography

Abaza, M. (2001). Shopping Malls, Consumer Culture and the Reshaping of Public Space in Eygpt. *Theory, Culture & Society, 18*(5), 97-114.

Aquinas, T. (1947). *Summa Theologica* (Vol. ii) New York: Benziger Bros.

Arendt, H. (1958). *The Human Condition.* Chicago, IL: University of Chicago Press.

——. (1959). A Reply to My Critics. *Dissent, 6*(2), 179-181.

——. (1964). *Eichmann in Jerusalem: A Report on the Banality of Evil.* New York: Viking.

——. (1967). *The Origins of Totalitarianism* (Third Edition). London: George Allen & Unwin Ltd.

——. (1968). *Between Past and Future.* New York: Viking.

——. (1970). *On Violence.* New York: Harvest, Harcourt & Brace.

——. (1971). Thinking and Moral Consideration: A Lecture. *Social Research, 38.*

——. (1972). *Crises of the Republic.* San Diego: Harvest/ Harcourt Brace Jovanovich.

——. (1973). *Men in Dark Times.* Hammondsworth: Penguin.

——. (1978a). *The Jew as Pariah: Jewish Identity and Politics in the Modern Age.* New York: Grove.

——. (1978b). *The Life of the Mind* (Vol. 1: Thinking). London: Secker and Warburg.

——. (1982). *Lectures on Kant's Political Philosophy.* Chicago: University of Chicago Press.

——. (1990). *On Revolution.* London: Penguin.

Bandura, A., & Walters, R. H. (1963). *Social Learning and Personality Development.* New York: Holt, Rinehart and Winston.

Barlow, J. P. (1996). A Declaration of the Independence of Cyberspace, from http://memex.org/barlow.html

Baudrillard, J. (1994). *Simulacra and Simulations.* Michigan: University of Michigan Press.

Bateson, G. (1987). *Steps to an Ecology of the Mind.* Northvale, NJ: Jason Aronson.

Benhabib, S. (1990). Hannah Arendt and the Redemptive Power of Narrative. *Social Research, 57*(1), 167-196.

——. (2002). Reversing the Dialectic of Enlightenment: The Reenchantment of the World. In J. P. McCormick (Ed.), *Confronting Mass Democracy and Industrial Technology* (pp. 343-360). Durham and London: Duke University Press.

Beniger, J. R. (1986). *The Control Revolution: Technological and Economic Origins of the Information Society*. Cambridge, MA: Harvard University Press.

Berelson, B., & Steiner, G. A. (1964). *Human Behaviour: an Inventory of Scientific Findings*. New York: Harcourt, Brace & World.

Berners-Lee, T. (2006). Interviews: Tim Berners-Lee. *developerWorks*. Retrieved 9 October, 2010 from http://www.ibm.com/developerworks/podcast/dwi/cm-int082206txt.html

Bickford, S. (2000). Constructing Inequality: City Spaces and the Architecture of Citizenship. *Political Theory, 28*(3), 355-376.

Bimber, B. (2000). The Study of Information Technology and Civic Engagement. *Political Communication, 17*(4), 329-333.

Bleyer, W. G. (1927). *History of American Journalism*. Boston: Houghton Mifflin.

Bob, C. (2002). Merchants of Morality. *Foreign Policy* (March/April), 36-45.

Brand, A. (1990). *The Force of Reason: An Introduction to Habermas' Theory of Communicative Action*. Sydney: Allen & Unwin.

Building Brands (2004). Marketing Definitions: Brand. Retrieved 5 April, 2004, from http://www.buildingbrands.com/definitions/02_brand_definition.shtml

Calhoun, C. (Ed.). (1992). *Habermas and the Public Sphere*. Cambridge MA: MIT Press.

Castells, M. (1996). *The Rise of the Network Society*. Cambridge, MA: Blackwell.

Castronova, E. (2007). *Exodus to the Virtual World: How Online Fun is Changing Reality*. New York: Palgrave Macmillan.

CIA, C. I. A. (2004). DCI Special Advisor Report on Iraq's WMD. Retrieved 1 May 2101, from https://www.cia.gov/library/reports/general-reports-1/iraq_wmd_2004/index.html

Cooke, M. (1997). Authenticity and Autonomy: Taylor, Habermas and the Politics of Recognition. *Political Theory, 25*(2), 258-288.

Cooper, S. (1997). Plenitude and Alienation: The Subject of Virtual Reality. In D. Holmes (Ed.), *Virtual Politics: Identity and Community in Cyberspace* (pp. 93-106). London: Sage.

Dalpino, C. E. (2001). Does Globalization Promote Democracy? An Early Assessment. *The Brookings Review, 19*(4), 45-48.

Dante, A. (1950). *On World Government* (Vol. 1). New York: Little Library of Liberal Arts.

Dean, J. (2001). Cybersalons and Civil Society: Rethinking the Public Sphere in Transnational Technoculture. *Public Culture, 13*(2), 243-265.

Debord, G. (1990). *Comments on the Society of the Spectacle* (M. Imrie, Trans.). London: Verso.

———. (1995). *The Society of the Spectacle* (D. Nicholson-Smith, Trans.). New York: Zone.

Deleuze, G. (1992). Postscript on Societies of Control. *October, 59*, 3-7.

Deleuze, G., & Guattari, F. (1987). *A Thousand Plateaus: Capitalism and*

Schizophrenia (B. Massumi, Trans.). Minneapolis: University of Minnesota Press.

Der Derian, J. (2001). *Virtuous War: Mapping the Military-Industrial-Media-Entertainment Network*. Boulder, CO: Westview.

Dewey, J. (1954). *The Public and its Problems*. Chicago, IL: Swallow.

Dupuy, J.-P. (1980). Myths of the Information Society. In K. Woodward (Ed.), *The Myths of Information: Technology and Postindustrial Society*. Madison, WI: Coda.

Flint, J. (2004). Insolent Chariots. *Forbes, 173*(6), 65.

Foucault, M. (1975). *Discipline and Punish: The Birth of the Prison*. New York: Random House.

——. (1978). *The History of Sexuality* (R. Hurley, Trans. Vol. 1). New York: Pantheon.

——. (1983). On the Genealogy of Ethics: An Overview of Work in Progress'. New York: Cambridge University Press. In H. Dreyfuss & P. Rainbow (Eds.), *Michel Foucault* (2nd ed.). Chicago, IL: University of Chicago Press.

Fraser, N. (1992). Rethinking the Public Sphere: A Contribution to the Critique of Actually Existing Democracy. In C. Calhoun (Ed.), *Habermas and the Public Sphere*. Cambridge, MA: MIT Press.

Gerbner, G., Gross, L., Morgan, M., & Signorielli, N. (1986). Living with Television: The Dynamics of the Cultivation Process. In J. Bryant & D. Zillman (Eds.), *Perspectives on Media Effects* (pp. 17-40). Hilldale, NJ: Lawrence Erlbaum.

Giddens, A. (1994). *Beyond Left and Right: The Future of Radical Politics*. Cambridge: Polity.

Global Footprint Network (2010). Footprint Basics—Overview Retrieved 7 October, 2010, from http://www.globalfootprint.org/

Goldhaber, M. H. (1997). The Attention Economy and the Net. *First Monday, 2*(4).

Goodchild, P. (1996). *Gilles Deleuze and the Question of Philosophy*. Madison: Fairleigh Dickinson University Press.

Grebowicz, M., & Merrick, H. (2011). *Beyond the Cyborg: Adventures with Haraway*. New York: Columbia University Press.

Gurevitch, M., & Blumler, G. (1990). Political Communication Systems and Democratic Values. In J. Lichtenberg (Ed.), *Democracy and the Mass Media*. New York: Cambridge University Press.

Habermas, J. (1970). A Theory of Communicative Competence. *Inquiry, 13*, 360-375.

——. (1976). *Zur Rekonstruktion des historischen Materialismus*. Frankfurt: Suhrkamp.

——. (1977). Hannah Arendt's Communications Concept of Power. *Social Research, 44*, 3-24.

——. (1983). Hannah Arendt: On the Concept of Power *Philosophical-Political*

Profiles (pp. 171-189). Cambridge, MA: MIT Press.

——. (1984). *The Theory of Communicative Action: Reason and the Rationalization of Society* (T. McCarthy, Trans. Vol. 1). Boston: Beacon.

——. (1987a). *The Philosophical Discourse of Modernity: Twelve Lectures* (F. Lawrence, Trans.). Cambridge, MA: MIT Press.

——. (1987b). *The Theory of Communicative Action: Lifeworld and System: A Critique of Functionalist Reason* (T. McCarthy, Trans. Vol. 2). Boston, MA: Beacon.

——. (1989). *The Structural Transformation of the Public Sphere: An Inquiry into a Category of Bourgeois Society* (T. Burger, Trans.). Cambridge: MIT Press.

——. (1990). *Moral Consciousness and Communicative Action* (C. Lenhardt, Trans.). Cambridge, MA: MIT Press.

——. (1992). Further Reflections on the Public Sphere. In C. Calhoun (Ed.), *Habermas and the Public Sphere*. Cambridge, MA: MIT Press.

——. (1993). *Autonomy and Solidarity: Interviews with Jurgen Habermas*: Verso.

——. (1994). Actions, Speech Acts, Linguistically Mediated Interactions and the Lifeworld. *Philosophical Problems Today*, *1*, 45-74.

——. (1996). *Between Facts and Norms: Contributions to a Discourse Theory of Law and Democracy* (W. Rehg, Trans.). Cambridge, MA: MIT Press.

——. (2002). Interview: A Conversation about Questions of Political Theory. In R. Von Schomberg & K. Baynes (Eds.), *Discourse and Democracy: Essays on Habermas's Between Facts and Norms*. Albany, NY: State University of New York Press.

——. (2006). Political Communication in Media Society: Does Democracy Still Enjoy an Epistemic Dimension? The Impact of Normative Theory on Empirical Research. *Communication Theory*, *16*(4), 411-426.

Hampson, R. (2007). Top 25 Biggest News Stories. *USA Today*, (14/9/07). Retrieved 25 October from http://www.usatoday.com/news/top25-headlines.htm

Haraway, D.J. (1991). A Cyborg Manifesto: Science, Technology, and Socialist Feminism in the Late Twentieth Century. in *Simians, Cyborgs and Women: The Reinvention of Nature* (pp. 149-181). New York: Routledge.

Hardin, G. (1968). The Tragedy of the Commons. *Science*, *162*(3859), 1243-1248.

Hardt, M., & Negri, A. (2000). *Empire*. Cambridge: Harvard University Press.

Harper, T. (2009). Smash the Strata! A Program for Techno-Political (r)Evolution. In D. Savat & M. Poster (Eds.), *Deleuze and New Technology*. Edinburgh: Edinburgh University Press.

Heidegger, M. (1973-74). The Anaximander Fragment. *Arion*, *1*(4), 576-626.

Horkheimer, M., & Adorno, T. (1987). *Dialectics of Enlightenment* (J. Cumming, Trans.). New York: Contiinuum.

Horowitz, I. L. (1999). Totalitarian Visions of the Good Society: Arendt. *Partisan Review*, *66*(2), 263-279.

Isaac, J. C. (1994). Oases in the Desert: Hannah Arendt on Democratic

Politics. *American Political Science Review, 88*(1), 156-168.

Jameson, F. (1991). *Postmodernism, or, The Cultural Logic of Late Capitalism.* Durham, NC: Duke University Press.

Jefferson, T. (1900). *The Jeffersonian Cyclopedia.* New York: Funk & Wagnalls.

Kant, I. (1985). 'Answering the Question: What Is Enlightnement?'. In H. Reiss (Ed.), *Kant's Political Writings.* Melbourne, Australia: Cambridge University Press.

Kellner, D. (2001). Globalisation, Technopolitics and Revolution. *Theoria* (Dec), 14-36.

Klein, N. (2000). *No Logo.* New York: Picador.

Kohn, M. (2001). The Mauling of Public Space. *Dissent, 48*(2), 71-77.

Kress, G. (1988). *Communication and Culture: An Introduction.* Sydney: New South Wales University Press.

Kristeva, J. (2001a). *Hannah Arendt* (R. Guberman, Trans.). New York: Columbia University Press,.

——. (2001b). *Hannah Arendt: Life is a Narrative.* Toronto: University of Toronto Press.

Lanchester, J. (2010). *Whoops! Why Everyone Owes Everyone and No One Can Pay.* London, New York: Allen Lane.

Love, N. S. (2002). Disembodying Democracy: Gendered Discourse in Habermas's Legalistic Turn. In J. P. McCormick (Ed.), *Confronting Mass Democracy and Industrial Technology* (pp. 321-342). Durham, NC: Duke University Press.

Luke, T. (1998). The Politics of Digital Inequality: Access, Capability and Distribution in Cyberspace. In C. Toulouse & T. W. Luke (Eds.), *The Politics of Cyberspace: A New Political Science Reader* (pp. 120-144). New York: Routledge.

Lyotard, J.-F. (1984). *The Postmodern Condition: A Report on Knowledge* (G. Bennington & B. Massumi, Trans.). Minneapolis, MN: University of Minnesota Press.

——. (1992). The Wall, the Gulf, and the Sun: A Fable. In M. Poster (Ed.), *Politics, Theory and Contemporary Culture.* New York: Columbia University Press.

Marcuse, H. (1964). *One Dimensional Man: Studies in the Ideology of Advanced Industrial Society* (2nd ed.). Boston, MA: Beacon.

——. (1968). *Negations.* Boston, MA: Beacon.

——. (no date). *Prospectus for One Dimensional Man.* Beacon Press archives.

Marx, K. (1973a). *Grundrisse* (M. Nicolaus, Trans.). New York: Vintage.

——. (1973b). Manifesto of the Communist Party. In D. Fernbach (Ed.), *Karl Marx: The Revolutions of 1848* (pp. 62-98). London: Penguin.

——. (1990). *Capital.* London: Penguin.

McCarthy, T. (1985). Complexity and Democracy, or the Seducements of Systems Theory. *New German Critique, 35,* 27-53.

McIntosh, W. V., & Cates, C. L. (1998). Hard Travellin': Free Speech in the

Age of the Information Super Highway. In C. Toulouse & T. W. Luke (Eds.), *The Politics of Cyberspace: A New Political Science Reader* (pp. 84-120). New York: Routledge.

McKenzie, E. (1994). *Privatopia: Homeowner Associations and the Rise of Residential Private Government*. New Haven: Yale University Press.

Mill, J. S. (1991). *On Liberty and Other Essays*. Oxford: Oxford University Press.

Moisy, C. (1997). Myths of the Global Information Village. *Foreign Policy, 107*(Summer), 78-87.

Monbiot, G. (2000a). *Captive State: The Corporate Takeover of Britain*. London: Macmillan.

——. (2000b). Dying of Consumption. Retrieved 15 April, 2004, from http://www.monbiot.com/

——. (2001). Privatising Our Minds. Retrieved April 4, 2004, from http://www.monbiot.com/

——. (2002). The Fake Persuaders. Retrieved April 14, 2004, from http://www.monbiot.com/

——. (2003). *The Age of Consent: A Manifesto for a New World Order*. London: Harper Perennial.

More, M. (1998). The Extropia Principles: A Transhumanist Declaration Version 3.0. Retrieved 13 May 2010 from http://www.maxmore.com/extprn3.htm

Mouffe, C. (2000a). *The Democratic Paradox*. London: Verso.

——. (2000b). For an Agonistic Model of Democracy. In N. O'Sullivan (Ed.), *Political Theory in Transition* (pp. 113-131). London: Routledge.

Negri, A. (1989). *The Politics of Subversion*. Oxford: Polity.

Nietzsche, F. (1956). The Genealogy of Morals (F. Golffing, Trans.) *The Birth of Tragedy and The Genealogy of Morals* (pp. 147-299). New York: Doubleday Anchor.

——. (1986). *Beyond Good and Evil* (W. Kaufmann, Trans.). New York: Vintage.

O'Sullivan, N. (2000). Power, Authority and Legitimacy: a critique of postmodern political thought. In N. O'Sullivan (Ed.), *Political Theory in Transition*. London: Routledge.

Olafson, F. A. (1990). Habermas as a Philosopher. *Ethics, 100*(3), 641-657.

Olesen, T. (2005). World Politics and Social Movements: the Janus Face of the Global Democratic Structure. *Global Society, 19*(2), 109-130.

Owen, D. S. (2002). *Between Reason and History: Habermas and the Idea of Progress*. Albany, NY: State University of New York Press.

Pahl, J. (2004). *Shopping Malls and Other Sacred Spaces: Putting God in Place*: Brazos.

Peters, T. (1997). What Great Brands Do. *Fast Company, August/September*.

Pitkin, H. F. (1998). *The Attack of the Blob: Hannah Arendt's Concept of the Social*. Chicago. IL: The University of Chicago Press.

Poster, M. (1994). A Second Media Age? *Arena, 3*, 49-92.

——. (1995). Postmodern Virtualities. In R. Burrows & A. Featherstone (Eds.), *Cyberspace, Cyberbodies, Cyberpunk* (pp. 79-96). London: Sage.

——. (1997). Cyberdemocracy: The Internet and the Public Sphere. In D. Holmes (Ed.), *Virtual Politics: Identity and Community in Cyberspace* (pp. 212-228). London: Sage.

Ralston Saul, J. (1997). *The Unconscious Civilization.* Hammondsworth: Penguin Books.

Rehg, W., & Bohman, J. (2002). Discourse and Democracy: The Formal and Informal Bases of Legitimacy in *Between Facts and Norms.* In R. Von Schomberg & K. Baynes (Eds.), *Discourse and Democracy: Essays on Habermas's Between Facts and Norms* (pp. 31-60). Albany, NY: State University of New York.

Research. (2010). *L'Oreal.* Retrieved 13 October, 2010, from http://www.loreal.com.au/_en/_au/index.aspx

Rheingold, H. (1993). *The Virtual Community: Homesteading of the Electronic Frontier.* Reading, MA: Addison-Wesley.

Robert, L. P., & Dennis, A. R. (2005). Paradox of Richness: A Cognitive Model of Media Choice. *IEEE Transactions on Professional Communication, 48*(1), 10-21.

Rose. (2000). Government and Control. *British Journal of Criminology, 40*(2).

Saco, D. (2002). *Cybering Democracy: Public Space and the Internet.* Minneapolis, MN: University of Minnesota Press.

Said, E. (1980). The Nation. *Islam Through Western Eyes*(April 26).

Sandel, M. (1982). *Liberalism and the Limits of Justice.* New York: Cambridge University Press.

Shah, D. V., Cho, J., Nah, S., Gotlieb, M. R., Hwang, H., Lee, N.-J., et al. (2007). Campaign Ads, Online Messaging, and Participation: Extending the Communication Mediation Model. *Journal of Communication, 57,* 676-703.

Sharma, P. (2008). Core Characteristics of Web2.0 Services. *Tech Pluto* Retrieved 5 October, 2010, from http://www.techpluto.com/web-20-services/

Sitton, J. F. (1987). Hannah Arendt's Argument for Council Democracy. *Polity, 20,* 80-100.

Sofoulis, Z. (2002). Cyberquake: Haraway's Manifesto. In G. Jahnert, K. Aleksander & K. Rosenbusch (Eds.), *Cyberfeminismus: Feministische Visionen mit Netz und ohne Boden?* (pp. 54-72). Berlin: Humboldt University.

Soros, G. (1998). *The Crisis of Global Capitalism: Open Society Endangered.* New York: Public Affairs.

Steinberg. (1958). *The Mass Communicators.* New York.

Streck, J. M. (1998). Pulling the Plug on Electronic Town Meetings: Participatory Democracy and the Reality of the Usenet. In C. Toulouse & T. Luke (Eds.), *The Politics of Cyberspace: A New Political*

Science Reader (pp. 18-47). New York: Routledge.

Sutherland, M. (1993). *Advertising and the Mind of the Consumer: What Works, What Doesn't and Why*. Sydney: Allen & Unwin.

Tett, G. (2009a). *Fool's Gold: How the Bold Dream of a Small Tribe at J.P. Morgan was Corrupted by Wall Street Greed and Unleashed a Catastrophe*. New York: Free Press.

——. (2009b). Icebergs and Ideologies: How Information Flows Fuelled the Financial Crisis. *Anthropology News*, (October), 6-7.

Toffler, A. (1990). *Powershift: Knowledge, Wealth, and Violence at the Edge of the 21st Century*. New York: Bantam.

Vidal, J. (1997). *McLibel: Burger Culture on Trial*. London: Macmillan.

Villa, D. (1997). Hannah Arendt: Modernity, Alienation, and Critique. In C. Calhoun & J. McGowan (Eds.), *Hannah Arendt and the Meaning of Politics* (pp. 179-207). Minneapolis, MN: University of Minnesota Press.

——. (2001). *Socratic Citizenship*. Princeton, NJ: Princeton University Press.

Waxman, J. (2000). *The Old 80/20 Rule Takes One on the Jaw: Internet Trends Report 1999 Review*. San Francisco: Alexa Res.

Wehner, P. (2001). Opinion: Ivory Arches and Golden Towers: Why We're All Consumer Researchers Now. *College English, 63*(3), 759-768.

White, H. (1987). *The Content of the Form: Narrative Discourse and Historical Representation*. London: The Johns Hopkins University Press.

Wilbur, S. (1997). An Archaeology of Cyberspaces: Virtuality, Community, Identity. In D. Porter (Ed.), *Internet Culture* (pp. 12-28). London: Routledge.

Wilde, O. (2005). The Soul of Man under Socialism. In J. M. Guy (Ed.), *The Complete Works of Oscar Wilde* (Vol. 4). Oxford: Oxford University Press.

Williagan, G. E. (1992). High Performance Marketing: An Interview with Nike's Phil Knight. *Harvard Business Review, July 1992*.

Wilson, M. (1997). Community in the Abstract: A Political and Ethical Dilemma. In D. Holmes (Ed.), *Virtual Politics: Identity and Community in Cyberspace* (pp. 145-162). London: Sage.

Wire services pick top stories of 1994. (1995). *Editor and Publisher, 128*(1), 54.

Wolf, N. (1991). *The Beauty Myth*. London: Vintage.

WWB. (2003, 1 May). What's Bigger than a Tom Ridge Press Conference? Retrieved 15 May 2010 from http://armedprophet.blogspot.com/2003_02_01_archive.html

Index